FOREWORD BY
THE WITCH OF THE FOREST

Goddess Stories

DISCOVER THEIR MYTHOLOGY

Alison Davies

ILLUSTRATIONS BY KATJA PEREZ

Foreword
by Lindsay Squire

I've been a Witch now for sixteen years, and for most of this time my practice was "secular" as I didn't work with gods or goddesses. But over the last three years my practice has evolved to one where I now work with deities, in particular the goddess Freya. I wish this book had been available back when I began to learn about and work with goddesses in my own Craft as it can be difficult to know where and how to start when you feel the pull to work and connect with a deity—but "Goddess Stories" is the perfect place to begin! It is fantastic for those at the start of their goddess journey as it introduces a wide variety of goddesses from a range of different pantheons, and is also valuable to those who have been working with goddesses in their craft for a while, but wish to deepen their relationship with their chosen deity.

I love how Alison has divided the book into four chapters representing each element, and the goddesses are arranged under the element they are aligned with. Alison shares stories about each goddess based on folklore which give a great introduction to a broad range of goddesses including from Celtic, Roman, Buddhist, Egyptian, Native American, and Norse mythology, as well as lesser known deities such as from Aztec and Sumerian folklore. Through the narratives the goddesses take on a life of their own and the reader can connect with their true essence. If you have an interest in a particular goddess you can use this as a starting point, and then branch out to explore other goddesses if you are drawn to them. I highly recommend this book to anyone who has an interest in goddesses. It goes beyond just being a collection of goddess folklore; rituals and affirmations will help you to connect with the goddesses on a deep and profound level. They help you to harness the power each goddess offers and bring their qualities into your life in a tangible way.

This book is also stunningly illustrated by Katja Perez, one of my favorite witchy artists. Katja's beautiful depiction of the goddesses, together with Alison's words, truly bring the goddess stories to life!

Wherever you are on your journey, prepare to unleash your inner goddess!

Introduction

How the deities came into being

Since the beginning of humanity, we have told stories. We have used them as a tool to explain why things happen in the world. We have used them to bond, and to understand each other and our differences. We have used them to entertain, and to heal. We looked at the sky and the stars above us, at the earth and our surroundings, and we saw all these magical things we didn't quite understand, and we made up tales to make sense of it all. And so, depending on where we were in the world, mythologies were formed, and they were influenced by our surroundings. Ideas sprang forth and the gods and goddesses were created.

These larger-than-life characters were based on us, on what we believed to be important attributes and gifts. While they were supernatural, they also offered us the opportunity to take a step back, to say, "This is not my doing, it is the will of the gods."

Their stories were a way of explaining why things happened and, when things didn't go our way, we could lay the blame firmly at their door. It makes sense that examining these characters and looking at their tales helps us better understand who we are, and our place in the world. We can also use their tales as a way of connecting with their unique energy.

Why goddesses?

Goddesses in particular are easily accessible. Unlike the gods who are often ego driven, the females of the species perform roles that we can identify with, which makes it easier for us to connect with them. They can be queens, mothers, homemakers, sisters, and best friends. They can be complex, or an open book, depending on their role in mythology, but always they are fascinating. They can help us understand ourselves and the world around us, and sometimes they can remind us that we, too, have powers and talents that we can put to good use.

Journey to the heart of the goddess and you will find a woman, sometimes wild and feral, a slave to her passions and driven by the well of love inside, sometimes brave—a warrior with a cause and the skill and strength to follow it up. She's a healer, too, wise beyond her years, with nimble fingers and the knowledge of eternity to soothe away hurt. Often, she's a mother, a creator, the font of all life, and while she gives birth to the universe, her mission is far from complete, for she cares too much. Let's not forget that she also wields a power more potent than any man, for while the gods may be the fathers, she is the "divine feminine," the womb, and the fertile seat of all ideas.

There is nothing that the goddess cannot do if she sets her mind to it, as we will explore in the pages of this book. It doesn't matter which area she governs, or the reach of her influence; if her heart is set on change, then change will happen and sometimes this is positive, sometimes negative, depending on the lesson she wants us to learn.

The narratives

The stories within hold a kernel of truth, some more than others are based on folklore, on tales that have been passed down orally for thousands of years. Some find their basis in the classics, in scholarly works that outline the exploits of the deities for that particular mythology; some are imagined narratives set around the chosen goddess and her themes and attributes. They are created to bring her to life, to allow her to step off the page and into your mind, so that you may connect with her true essence.

You'll also find that some of the tales are similar—this is because mythologies around the world share ideas and concepts, and often borrow from each other to build a common landscape. Cultures cross over, and each deity has a counterpart, a sister from another mythological mister, and so themes and tales are often duplicated. But while there is common ground, each goddess remains distinctly different and there is something for everyone. Depending on your interests, and where you are in your life right now, you are sure to find one that appeals.

How to use this book

As for the stories, some will resonate more than others, some will simply amuse and entertain, then there will be those that empower you, or strike a chord and make you want to read them again and again. How you choose to use this book is up to you. If you're drawn to a particular mythology, you may wish to single out deities from that area and read those tales first. If you're looking to connect with a goddess for a specific reason, you may wish to choose by looking at the themes highlighted at the beginning of the tale. If you just want to enjoy everything on offer, you can read from start to finish or dip in at your leisure.

The book is split into four sections, each one highlighting an element and a different aspect of the goddess, to make it easy for you to identify them. You may discover through your choice of stories that you have an affinity with a particular type of deity. Whatever draws you to a goddess is reason enough to read her story and connect with her at a deeper level.

The practical ritual at the end of each tale is there to help you harness the energy of that deity. It's a way of taking the themes and qualities associated with her and bringing them into your daily life. It should help you engage with her story and unleash your inner goddess by developing certain skills and attributes. The affirmations offer a quick goddess fix that you can apply anytime and anywhere, to feel empowered.

Once you've read the story, take a moment to digest what happened and how it made you feel. Then if you'd like to take it further and tap into the specific energy of the deity, practice the ritual, and repeat the affirmation throughout the day, to strengthen your connection.

Ultimately, what you have in your hands is a story book, and an introduction to goddesses from around the world. It's a way of getting to know them through their narratives and understanding the deeper themes at work. It's also a way of getting to know yourself, of understanding where you sit in the world, and how you, too, can develop goddess power and bring it into your life every day. It's time to acknowledge and embrace the "divine feminine" in the world, and to enjoy delving deeper into the magical tales behind the goddesses.

Earth and Mother

Within this section you'll find earth and mother goddesses, characters who are strong and grounded, and sometimes groundbreaking. Wise women and sages, primordial and primal, these deities are the ones you'll find standing at the dawn of time. They created the world and everything in it, stepping out of chaos and bringing a sense of surety and calm. They're the mother goddesses, the nurturing souls who cannot help but intervene, because they only want the best. Sometimes they're overprotective to the point of being stifling, but like all good moms they also know when to step back or lead by example.

They're the nature spirits, too, the ones who have an affinity with wildlife and the environment, and can help us to be the same. In some cases, they are the landscape, or the shifting seasons that color the vista. They're the changes, big and small, and they reveal the cyclical nature of life upon the earth through their stories and actions.

They can help you stand your ground and find your feet, create the world around you, and connect with others. Let them be your anchor and your inspiration, for their advice is timeless and true.

Atira

Native American Earth Goddess

THEMES
Abundance, creativity, new growth, inspiration

"THE CORN MOTHER"

When the Great Spirit of many Native American and First Nations mythologies made the earth, he made it possible for the people to live off the land and live together in harmony. He made it so the humans could share this space with all the other creatures and live happily side by side. He showed them the old ways and the things they must do for their families to flourish, and he made it clear that this was how it was meant to be.

"The earth does not belong to you," he said, "you only borrow it during your lifetime."

And while many of the tribes followed this creed and took it to their hearts, there were some who thought they were above the gods, some who thought they *were* the gods, and some who acted like it. As time went on, these people became more and more frustrated. Their need for power and one-upmanship drove them to terrible deeds and they began to destroy the very thing that sustained them. They cared little for the environment and the animals they shared it with, and even less for each other. They believed there were other ways to survive and thrive, which didn't involve taking time, effort, and care to nurture the land. The resentment they had for those who did grew, and grew, and what started like a tiny anthill of annoyance became a great stone mountain of hate.

"You must do something," the ancestral spirits urged the Great Spirit. "If you leave them to their ways, they will destroy the earth and each other, and there will be nothing left." The Great Spirit agreed. He could see what was happening and knew it was time for action, so he planted a seed in the heavens, a seed born of light and goodness. Then he sent word to the medicine men and women that

those who cared should retreat to a cave in the west where they would be safe from harm. Once all the people had gathered in the giant cave in the middle of the mountain, the entrance was sealed and the Great Spirit set to work.

Taking an almighty breath, he poured his spirit into the rivers and streams, until they flowed freely as one. They surged through the land and, as the waters began to rise, they swallowed huge swathes of earth and swept the evildoers to their doom. On and on they rolled, a force to be reckoned with. Only those within the cave were safe. Once the floods had cleansed the earth of all the badness, the Great Spirit rolled away the stone at the entrance to the cave and set his people free. But this time, to ensure they stayed on the straight and narrow, and to help nurture their spiritual strength, he employed the assistance of Atira, the corn mother he had grown from seed in the heavens.

Just like the seed, and an ear of corn, she was sweet and imbued with lightness; she was a goddess who could sustain both the spirit and the physical body. She was also strong and able to nurture new growth and encourage her people to cultivate the same strength and lightness in themselves. But her lessons didn't end there, for Atira was not just a farmer of souls, but of the land too. She knew how to care for the crops and ensure that they grew in abundance, and this she taught to the people.

She was the one they called upon when the earth was barren, and nothing would grow. She was the one who would send the rains to drench the soil, and the sun to welcome the first new shoots. She was the one they dreamed about when times were tough, and they needed inspiration.

And so Atira became the mother of every living thing, the corn lady, and the one who would always provide, and this she did by leaving a legacy. Wherever her feet had touched the earth, great fields of golden corn grew. They stretched to the heavens, and acted as a conduit, bringing her and her people closer together.

GODDESS AFFIRMATION

"With every step I take, I am connected to earth energy."

GODDESS RITUAL

Atira is an inspiring earth goddess. She encourages new growth and leads by example. In her earthly guise she is the golden sheaths of corn that grow in abundance. Her mission is to sustain and promote positive energy. Caring for the environment is the best way to connect to her power, and to attract prosperity.

This ritual, which works with the earth and the concept of growth, helps to lift the spirits and generate positive energy.

If you have access to a plot of land, whether that's your backyard, or a community garden that you can cultivate, then you can use it for this exercise. If you're limited on outdoor space, invest in a couple of planters or pots.

- Depending on your preference and the space you have, choose some vegetable or flower seeds. If you're struggling for inspiration, opt for wildflowers, which are easy to grow and ideal for bees and other pollinators.

- Prepare the soil by removing any stones or weeds. If you're using a planter, fill most of the way up with potting soil.

- Dip your hands into the earth and feel the moist soil between your fingers as you fashion a trough or space for your seeds to grow.

- Breathe deeply and draw this earth energy into your heart.

- Scatter your seeds into the soil. As you do, ask the earth to replenish your spirit and bless you with new growth in any area of your life.

- Cover over with the remaining soil, then water liberally.

- As you water, picture the seeds growing into beautiful blooms or vegetable plants.

- Say, "I nurture abundance and new growth."

- Every time you water the seeds, repeat this affirmation, and give thanks for earth's abundant, life-giving energy.

Elen of the Ways

Celtic Goddess of Pathways

THEMES
Guidance, shamanism, magic, nature

"THE PATH THAT LEADS YOU HOME"

At the dawn of time, she stepped out of the shadows. She sprang forth like a young sapling, ready to greet the sun and embrace her destiny. She grew with the landscape. Her limbs were strong and sun-kissed like the branches of an oak, and they reached for the stars. Her hair was red and tousled, braided with vines and leaves, and left to fall about her shoulders like a cloak. Her eyes were the brightest green to match the undergrowth and the new shoots and shrubs that came to life all around her. Most striking of all were the antlers that twisted from her brow, like a crown of bone. They marked her out as special. This was no ordinary woman. This was Elen of the Ways, wild and sacred, a goddess of the earth.

Over the years many searched for her, Celtic warriors and Roman emperors alike, but while they might have glimpsed her in between the trees or heard the rustle of her skirts as she ran, they could never be sure that it wasn't just a dream, for Elen walked the dreamworld, too.

One night a young hunter happened to find himself wandering the woods. He had lost track of time and, as the veil of night drew in, he cocooned himself in the trunk of a tree. The sounds of the forest filled him with fear—the ghostly creak of timber above his head, the whooshing of wind as it rattled the leaves and branches. The shuffling, snuffling sounds of the very creatures he had longed to catch in the height of the afternoon sun now made him shiver. He was cold and alone, with nowhere to run.

Gritting his teeth, he pulled his thin cloak about his shoulders and curled into a tight ball. He was about to close his eyes, to pray for the sanctuary of sleep, when something caught his attention—two flickers of light within the darkness, like tiny flames, but brighter.

He watched, transfixed as the dancing lights moved up ahead, then he realized they were the eyes of an antlered deer burning bright in the darkness. Stumbling to his feet, he felt compelled to follow and began to creep through the forest floor. The beast did not run as he might have expected. Instead it seemed to slow down, as if it wanted him to get close.

"How strange!" he thought, and yet he felt oddly comforted by its presence.

Onward through the gnarled branches he crept, keeping a short distance between himself and the animal. He had never seen a deer like it; it was a reindeer and not a common sight in the woods at that time. It felt like the creature was leading him, as if they were tethered by an invisible stream of light that passed between them.

Every so often the deer would stop, turn its head delicately, and let its soft gaze fall upon the man, and in those moments he would feel a calmness settle inside. Sometimes he even thought he heard a word, just one word, "home," and he wondered if the deer was letting him know that this ancient forest was its home, or whether it was telling him to go home.

Eventually, there was a clearing, a break in the dense cluster of woodland, and the sight of a path the hunter recognized. He stumbled into the space, turning to look once more at the deer, but in its place stood a woman, a magnificent antlered being with a waterfall of berry-red hair and glistening green eyes.

She pointed toward the path with a slender finger.

"Home." She smiled, and then she motioned to the woods. "Home," she whispered again, and he understood.

As the sun began to rise, the vision before him faded. The hunter stirred from slumber to find he was no longer nestled in a tree trunk. He was lying upon a dusty path and the woods were behind him. He rubbed at his eyes and scratched his head.

"Was it a dream? But then how am I here?" He scrambled to his feet and peered again into the heart of the forest. In the deep, earthy recesses he thought he saw movement, a smile and twinkling green eyes, antlers and hooves, which turned and bolted in the opposite direction.

"Home," he said and let the words drift upon the breeze.

From that day onward, the young man set aside his hunting way, no longer chasing forest creatures for fun but going out of his way to care for them. He trailed through the woods doing his bit for nature, looking for the mysterious antlered woman who had helped him find the right path, but he never found her again.

"I choose the right path for me."

GODDESS RITUAL

A visionary who knows that there are many journeys in life, from the physical to the emotional and spiritual, Elen is a nurturing goddess. Linked to the earth and the wild woods, she is a guide who can help you discover your life's purpose.

This ritual uses a visual narrative to help you connect with the natural world and your innate intuition. You'll need a journal and pen to record any insights.

* Find a comfortable place to sit, then breathe deeply and close your eyes.

* Visualize yourself sitting at the heart of the woods, with your back resting against a tree.

* Feel the bark against your skin and let your bodyweight sink into the trunk.

* Every breath you take connects you more deeply with the environment.

* You notice movement up ahead. You can see the undergrowth parting, and there, between the trees, is a young deer.

* It moves forward slowly, until it is standing before you. At this point you might want to reach out and touch the deer, or even speak a silent greeting in your mind.

* Let your imagination take over and communicate in a way that feels right with your animal guide. If you're looking for guidance, ask the deer for help.

* When you're ready, let the deer go, take a few deep breaths, and open your eyes.

* Record any insights, messages, or visual clues for future reference.

Gaia

THEMES
Birth and rebirth, balance,
the cycles of life

**"HOW THE WORLD
WAS BORN"**

In the beginning, there existed chaos; an idea stirring and not yet formed, an empty chasm where anything could happen. For isn't that what chaos means—the potential of something, be it trouble, destruction, joy, or madness? This was at the heart of where it all began. The world did not exist, and neither did the heavens. There was nothing and there was everything if you had the imagination to see it.

Chaos was timeless—the serpent that swallowed its own tail, it seemed never-ending, and probably would have gone on forever if it hadn't been for Gaia. Where she came from no one knows, but it was out of chaos that she was born. Like a shooting star, she shattered the darkness and brought new life in the form of the earth, a planet which sat in the center of the gaping maw of the sky.

And slowly, the burning rock that was at the heart of her passion for every living thing began to spin. And with every turn, it grew in size and shape and the beautiful mother goddess stepped into her power. She took her place in the vista of the universe, claimed Mount Olympus as her own and sat upon the heavenly throne.

Next came Tartarus, lord of the Underworld, to watch over the place beneath the earth where the souls of the dead would rest. Then came love in the shape of Eros, for without love, there is nothing, and the world would eventually cease to exist. Gaia knew this, and so she knew that he would have to come next if she were to survive and thrive. These three became a cosmic force, and the earliest of deities to help fashion the world. They were a team united in what they could achieve, and they ruled together.

But Gaia was not meant to simply exist. It was her natural urge to create, to give birth; she was the mother

of everything and yet she had no children to call her own. After a while, hundreds of thousands of lifetimes at the very least, Gaia grew restless and lonely. She was tired of talking to herself, of being the light of everything but the mother of nothing. And so, in her desperation and to feed her need to nurture, she created Uranus. He would be her confidante, her partner in all things, and he would govern the sky and the heavens.

Alongside him, and to keep them both company, she created Pontus to look after the oceans and Ourea who was assigned the mountains and hills. So the world began to take shape. Great swathes of landscape were formed, crafted by the blink of a godly eye. The seas flowed at the flick of a hand; the salty waters carved their own path through the land to create islands. The sky above pressed down, kissing the earth with its life-giving breath, and there was hope for the future. Gaia saw and felt this, but still there was more to do.

Taking Uranus as her lover, together they sired Cronus, who would go on to be the mightiest of gods, and the first of the Titans. But while you might imagine their firstborn would be kind of heart and willing to play his part in the creation of the world, Cronus was troubled and held a deep disregard for his mother. He became the god of time, but his version of time was destructive, a devouring force that would eventually be toppled by the introduction of the Olympians.

Gaia for her part continued to do what mothers do; she loved and nurtured each creation. She gave birth to night and day, and a myriad of other aspects, and most importantly she gave birth to her people, making the stars in the sky, and the sun to show them the way. In return she was adored and exalted. Whether she appeared as an old woman whose body was the earth, and whose head was crowned by the starry skies, or as a voluptuous maiden laid bare to shape the land, Gaia was the bringer of calm, the one who had stepped forth out of chaos, the mother of everything—*she* was how the world was born.

"Every day is a new beginning and an opportunity to create my world."

GODDESS RITUAL

Gaia is the earth, she is the start of everything, and at the heart of the cycles of life. She has the power to create and shape new things. Her life-giving energy brings countless blessings.

This ritual taps into earth energy, so that you can feel grounded and ready to face each new day, making the most of opportunities that come your way.

This ritual is best performed in the morning, if possible, at sunrise or when you first get up.

✳ Stand outside on the grass barefoot. Keep your feet hip-width apart, and your shoulders back.

✳ Let your weight drop into your lower legs and bend your knees slightly.

✳ Feel the connection you have to the earth. Feel it through the soles of your feet.

✳ Close your eyes and notice how the blades of grass curl around your feet.

✳ Take a deep breath in and as you exhale, imagine tiny roots growing from your soles, stretching deep into the ground. Imagine them curling around other roots beneath the surface, anchoring you to the earth.

✳ Drop your weight down and feel that connection strengthen.

✳ Imagine that with every breath, you draw even more earth energy into your body; it travels along the root system and up through your feet.

✳ Feel that energy surge through your body, refreshing and recharging you for the day ahead.

Spider Grandmother

Native American Earth Goddess

THEMES
Psychic power, vision, reassurance, insight

"ESCAPE TO SPIDER ROCK"

Timeless and ancient, Spider Grandmother is the oldest of elders. Like the dusty, rocky surface of her homeland, she bears cracks in her skin, her hands worn dry. Her hair is as black as the darkest winter night, and her skin is tinged the golden amber of the sands she walks on. But her eyes are bright and piercing, full of clear vision; they can see into your heart and your future.

Some say she lives in a hole in the ground, spinning her webs and scuttling around, while some believe that Spider Rock is where she rests her head. This tall, jutting pinnacle is the perfect place for her to sit and view the world. The mountain is dry and whitened from the bones of those who have gone before, and the children who have dared to enter her realm—Spider Grandmother does not take kindly to intruders. At least that's what they say in all the stories, whispered tales told around billowing campfires. It's no wonder young warriors avoid climbing to the top. After all, it does not do to incur the wrath of an earth goddess.

But then there are some who cannot help it. Like the young Dene warrior, chased by a war party from an enemy tribe while out scouting for food. Caught unawares by the lake splashing water upon his face, he ran for what seemed like miles, dodging the arrows, darting behind rocks and bushes, looking for a way out. And still they chased him. They could smell his fear, and they knew that his legs could not carry him forever.

The boy pushed on, but his limbs were tired, and his mouth was dry. The midday heat burned through his skin, and even the sweat upon his brow had dried up. It was only a matter of time before an arrow would puncture his flesh, or he would collapse from exhaustion. The boy did not wish to let his tribe down, but he couldn't think of a

way out. So as he blundered on, he prayed with all his might to the earth deities that relief or death would come swiftly.

It was then that he encountered the tallest rock he had ever seen. It stood like a plinth rising up from the earth and he wondered if it had once been a giant, or some other monstrous being turned to stone. He stopped in his tracks, for there was no way he could climb it. He could hear the party picking up speed, the hooves of their horses getting closer. This was surely the end for him. But then, just when he had given up hope, a silken thread slid down the side of the rock. He watched it glinting in the sunlight. It was so delicate it would surely not hold his weight and yet there it was, dancing before his eyes.

He reached for it and tugged at the end. It was strong and springy. Quickly he wrapped it around his waist and began to climb. The thread held him firm and even pulled him upward. Soon he was staggering, scaling the jagged stone at an incredible speed, until he reached the top and fell forward into what looked like a giant eagle's nest. He lay and stretched out his hands. He could feel drops of dew nestled in craters upon the surface and he drank deep of the fresh water. Below, he heard the cries of the war party. They did not know where he was. He listened as

they went upon their way, and was about to scramble up, but a voice stopped him.

"Would you be going without saying thank you for my hospitality?"

He looked up and found himself gazing into an old woman's face.

"I am Spider Grandmother," she said, offering a gnarled hand, "and this is my home." The young warrior looked in astonishment as the woman before him seemed to shift and change, from spider to human to something in between, but all the time she smiled and there was no malice to the expression. Suddenly it all made sense; the silken thread she had spun, and the way she had come to his aid after he'd prayed to the gods. He thanked her from the bottom of his heart, and they talked. She showed him how she lived, and how she helped the tribes by spinning their fates and showering them with blessings. She filled him up with wisdom, and when the time came, she helped him down the side of the mountain with her thread.

When the young man returned to his tribe, he told them of his meeting with Spider Grandmother, and how she'd helped him in his hour of need. And from that day onward, no longer was she the scary, fiendish old lady of the tales, but an earth mother and friend to the Dene people.

"I have clear vision and use my senses to see beneath the surface."

GODDESS RITUAL

Spider Grandmother is a kindly old woman, even though she is feared by some. Wise and perceptive, this earth goddess uses both her objectivity and her intuition to get to the heart of the matter.

This ritual uses the stones of the earth to help you create an oracle that can be used to heighten your intuitive senses.

You will need to collect a handful of smooth stones that you like the look of, and a permanent marker pen.

✳ Start by cleaning and polishing the stones so that you have a clear surface to work with.

✳ Next, think of different inspirational words to write on the stones, for example you might have "hope," "strength," "joy," "clarity," and so on.

✳ Write each word on a stone and let it dry in the sun.

✳ Use the oracle each morning. Hold the stones in both hands. Close your eyes and breathe deeply.

✳ Imagine you are imbued with earth energy, then ask for an insight or some inspiration for the day ahead.

✳ Place the stones on the floor, continuing to keep your eyes closed, then pick one.

✳ Open your eyes and read your word of the day.

Áine

Celtic Goddess of Summer and Wealth

THEMES
Respect, honor, wisdom, wealth

"A FAIR TRADE"

It has been said that you should never cross the fair of face, or she who is of fairy race, and both together is a charm, for you will surely come to harm.

Never has that saying been more true than with the Celtic goddess Áine. Queen of the Fairies and fairest of all, she was filled with love and sunshine—summer reigned true when she came down from above. Midsummer was her time to rule; on the longest day and night she would share her radiant light, and her gift of abundance. Her people were truly grateful for she gave birth to the grain and encouraged its growth, and when two people met it was Áine's gentle magic that stirred the first embers of love.

Such a being of beauty, it is no surprise that she was desired, for in her eyes you could see the sun rise and, in her smile, the sweetest flowers of summer opened their petals to shine. But it was a foolish man who would underestimate her strength, thinking she was as delicate as those first buds in spring. Her fairy heritage alone should have filled the lustiest lad with caution, for it does not do to challenge the fay.

There is always one, and in this case it was one who thought he was above the law. Ailill was his name, and he was the King of Munster. Being of such supreme sovereignty you might think he was blessed with a degree of wisdom, but like most humans he had frailties too, and the problems didn't stop there. He had noticed his fields were barren, the grass was dry and brittle, and the crops were failing. His livestock were falling ill from lack of food, his people would soon follow suit, and so he consulted a druidess for help. She urged him to go to the Knockainey on Halloween and seek the advice of the deities.

The young king knew little of the gods, but having no other way to solve the problem, decided to take this path. On his arrival he was overcome by lethargy. So tired was he that he fell into a deep and magical slumber, and it was in this state that he met Áine. She came in the guise of a red mare, and then as the breeze blew, she transformed into a young maiden with rosy-red cheeks, and a cloak to match the color of her blushes.

"You must tend to the fields with love and care. I can show you how for I am the goddess Áine, and this is my gift," she said, smiling.

But the king wasn't listening, he had forgotten the reason for his presence. He was transfixed by her charms and overcome with lust. He reached out with his arms and pulled her to him. Despite her protests, he forced himself upon her. Blinded by the moment, and the passion in his heart, he forgot who he was dealing with until it was too late.

Áine instantly took her revenge. She bit down hard upon his ear, tearing it from his head and casting it to the ground. As the blood poured from the ragged wound, the king realized to his cost just what this meant. For it was the law in Ireland at that time that only one unblemished could rule the kingdom.

"You have maimed me!" he cried. "And now I am nothing, I have lost my crown and my power. I have lost everything!"

"You didn't listen," she replied, "and you dared to touch me, thinking you could have your way. For your ego I take your ear and I take your sovereignty. It is a fair trade." And in that moment the die was cast, and Áine would become known for her vengeful streak, as well her immense kindness. Those who followed her ways would always be sure to pay her the respect she deserved. They would burn enormous fires at midsummer in her honor and spread the ashes over the fields to ensure both her blessing and a bountiful harvest.

As for the dishonored king, he became known as Aulom, meaning "one-eared," and, despite his deeds, his descendants flourished to become a powerful Irish dynasty, known as the Eóghanachta.

But the story was never forgotten, as it never should be.

For when you cross the fair of face or one who's born of fairy race, you disrespect Áine's timeless charm, and you will surely come to harm.

Áine

"I treat myself and others with respect and care."

GODDESS RITUAL

Fiery Áine is associated with the sun and the moon, and also the earth. A benevolent deity, she rewards those who treat her with respect by giving generously. She is associated with wealth, being the goddess who gave birth to the grain, which feeds and sustains. She knows that true beauty shines when you treat yourself and others with respect, and honor the land.

This ritual, which works with the sun's light and fairy magic, will help you develop a sense of respect for yourself, the world around you, and those you engage with.

 At midday the sun is at the height of its powers, so it's the ideal time to pay your respects to the earth and leave an offering for the nature spirits. Grain is associated with Áine, and so it is the perfect gift, which will benefit the birds and other animals, too.

 Gather grain in a bowl.

 Take this outside around midday and scatter the grain on the ground. If you prefer, you can take a walk in your local park and scatter the grain under a tree, or in a river for the ducks and geese to eat.

 As you do this, you might want to say a little prayer or make a wish. Think about what you truly value about yourself and your life and give thanks for that.

 Also think about your surroundings and all the things you appreciate, like the beautiful scenery, the creatures you share the earth with, and the sun that lights the sky. Be aware of all the things that deserve your respect.

Coatlicue

Aztec Mother Goddess

THEMES
Fertility, renewal, regeneration, balance

"THE SNAKE WOMAN"

Slowly moving her rippling form, she slithers from between the cracks, working her way up from the belly of the earth where she has nestled for an eternity. Her scales are smooth and etched with intricate patterns; they come together and form new shapes with each sinewy movement. She does not need to rush, or struggle. To her, life is a perfectly timed dance and she is in control. She wraps around boulders, smoothing against the rock. She slides with little effort, curving around any obstacle in her path. She knows that you do not need to be forceful to have your way; a caress holds as much power as a deadly bite, but you would do well to avoid either from her. It's true to say that if you saw her, you might be alarmed, but her snake-like form does not reveal her true nature. She wears the skin of a predator for a reason. She wants you to be wary, to realize that she can inflict pain if she needs to.

She is Coatlicue, snake woman, and earth goddess; a creator and destroyer, mother of gods and mortals, and so many other things, and this is her time. She has waited for thousands of years to reveal her true self, and it is only now, with you, that she feels ready.

Wearing her two faces, both of which are fanged serpents to represent the two sides of her psyche, she crawls into your world from the pages of this book. Her duality is what makes her special, for she believes there are two sides to everything—light and dark, day and night, summer and winter, all opposing forces that work together.

And if you look more closely you will notice her shape bleeds from one image to another; sometimes she looks like a woman and sometimes a snake. Her skirt shifts around her ankles. Its fluid movement is a mirage, for

while it looks like it is made up of the silvery strands of the sea, it is in fact comprised of snakes; thousands of slithery creatures wriggling in unison. It's a symbol of her fertility—after all, she gave birth to the earth and everything upon it.

Do not be scared, for while her fingers and toes are shaped like claws, they are simply there to help her deal with the changing landscape. She is equipped for rough terrain, should her trek into your subconscious mind require it. Yes, she is here to enter your dreams, and take you on a journey, for Coatlicue likes to lead.

She is called Toci, meaning "our grandmother," another aspect to her personality, but while most elders are frail and peaceful, she feeds on the corpses of the dead. This might alarm you; these are hardly the actions of a sweet old lady, but this is her way of showing you that the earth consumes all that dies. It replenishes its resources by absorbing the bodies, in order to grow and evolve. It is a process of renewal, just as the snake sheds its many skins, and Coatlicue wants to show you that life is a series of small deaths and rebirths. There is nothing to fear.

She wears a necklace made of hearts and hands, and a skull—a symbol of her strength and power over life and death. And while she wears these things as tokens, they also represent the hearts and hands that she holds dear, the bodies that come to her after their time on earth is spent.

You may wonder why she wanders the earth, seeping into the minds of dreamers just like you. You may think she has come to take you away, as she twists her undulating curves around the world and around your heart. Perhaps she is here to teach you a lesson, or to give you a vision of the future?

The answer is simpler than that. She is primarily a mother goddess, and her mission is to find her son, the god of war. She predicted his fate long ago, for destiny is a part of her domain and she knew exactly when the fall of the Aztec Empire would occur. Whether he listened to her or not is another matter, but ever since she has wanted to be reunited with him.

So, if you do see her upon these pages, in your mind as you drift into slumber, or even gliding in her snake-like guise across your path, do not be afraid. Instead, give her some room to move, let her dance before your eyes and meander where she needs to be.

She is Coatlicue, the snake woman; a mother, a grandmother and, like all women upon the earth, a creative life-giving force.

"Every breath replenishes my soul and allows me to regenerate."

GODDESS RITUAL

Fertility is a key theme for this goddess, whether you're birthing humans, new ideas or, in Coatlicue's case, the earth, the idea is that you can produce something from nothing. She changes shape and form and is able to regenerate by casting off the skin of her previous incarnations.

This ritual uses the symbolism of the snake, to help you reinvent yourself and feel empowered and renewed.

* Start by finding a spot where you can lay upon the earth, preferably on a patch of grass. Spend a few minutes breathing deeply to relax your body and mind.

* Turn your attention to your limbs and press them deeper into the earth. You might notice blades of grass tickling your skin, or the cool dampness of the soil beneath you.

* Press your body into the earth and feel the connection that you have.

* Take a deep breath in, and, as you exhale, imagine casting off all those things causing you pain or anguish, from small worries and concerns to any stress or tension gathered in your body and mind.

* As you inhale, imagine drawing in the replenishing energy of the earth.

* Continue to breathe in this way for a few minutes.

* When you're ready, slowly rise to your feet, as if you've stepped out of your old skin, to emerge refreshed and ready to reinvent yourself.

Eostre

Celtic Goddess of the Dawn and Spring

THEMES
New beginnings, growth, hope, the cycles of life

"THE SONGBIRD AND THE HARE"

A long, long time ago, when the ancient forests covered the earth, and the seas merged into one, there lived a beautiful goddess called Eostre. Her smile was like a warm spring day, and she sprinkled her laughter like the first drops of dew upon the meadows. When she walked it was with such lightness that her delicate footsteps caused wildflowers to bloom whenever they touched the ground. Clothed in the colors of the season, she would blend in with her surroundings making it difficult for you to spot her, but she was always there, in among the bluebells and the tall trees. Her grass-green skirts would swish like a gentle breeze as she moved, for she loved nothing more than to watch nature unfold.

To her, each day was an opportunity to start again and enjoy a new beginning. She recognized the cycles of life and knew that there was a time for everything. Just as the spring would herald her arrival, it would eventually blend into summer, and she would fade away. Then came fall with its brisk winds and golden glow, swiftly followed by the starker, harsher months of winter. Each phase held potential and would roll on to the next. It was a never-ending circle, which the goddess took to her heart.

For her part, she enjoyed spring the most, and not just because it was her time to reign supreme. She felt it was the season with the most potential for new growth. She could see it all around her, the buds unfurling, peeking their tiny heads toward the sky to steal a glimpse of sunlight; they were tiny nuggets with colorful secrets inside. She watched the grass growing straight and true, and the trees with their first coat of leaves. Spring, for her, was a hint at what was to come, and she found it all so exciting.

So, when she spied a poor frozen songbird beneath a giant oak, it weighed heavy on her heart. This was not a time for death but a time to be reborn. She had been trailing through the woods as she did every day, letting her fingers linger over bark and burr, skipping over the exposed roots, as she made her way to the glade where the sun shone the brightest. The bird had stopped Eostre in her tracks, its tiny, speckled form preserved by the ice that had come before. Its chest was still plump and brightly patterned, but there was no tender rise and fall, no movement at all.

Crouching down, she brushed her finger over the damp feathers.

"Oh sweet bird, this is not what I wish for you," she whispered, for indeed she was the goddess of new life, of beginnings and not endings.

She picked up the lifeless body and cradled it in her arms. While she could not bring it back to life, she could transform it—after all, that was what spring was about: transition, change, and a fresh start.

"Little bird so lost in sleep, for your soul I wholly weep. A new beginning I bring to bear, breathe again but as a hare." Slowly, surely, a shimmering shifting occurred as she spoke the words. The tiny bird grew bigger and stronger. No longer cloaked in feathers, she wore fur, and her ears were long and pointy. Her eyes were still bird-bright and clear, and her spirit shared qualities from both creatures.

When the transformation was done, the hare sat before the goddess Eostre, and she spoke into her mind, as most animals do.

"Goddess, how can I ever thank you for giving me new life?"

"You do not need to," Eostre replied. "It is my gift to you, little one."

"Then I must give you a gift," the hare continued, "something special to mark the occasion and the time of year." The goddess watched as the hare that had once been a bird, and was still avian in part, produced a selection of brightly colored, glistening eggs. She had never seen anything as enchanting, and she whooped with delight at the sparkling offerings before her.

"These are for you," said the hare. "They are Eostre's eggs, and they will forever be called by that name." The goddess smiled. "This is a fine gift, and I am grateful." And indeed she was, so much so that the tradition continued for many years, and still does to this day, just as Eostre comes with the spring and plays among the tall trees and flowering meadows. Then, when the time is right, she passes on to the next season and the cycle goes on. Every time she visits, she brings her eggs with her—a gift from the hare and a symbol of renewal.

"Each new cycle of life brings hope and adventure."

GODDESS RITUAL

Eostre is synonymous with new beginnings, and growth. She is part of the cycle of life and understands that there is a flow and an order to everything. An open-hearted deity, she is ready to embrace whatever comes, and she can show us how to breathe new life into any situation.

This ritual works with the invigorating energy of the earth, to imbue you with hope and enthusiasm.

* Find a meadow, field, or area with wildflowers where you can sit and relax.

* If possible, choose first thing in the morning, when everything still feels fresh. If the grass is damp, take a blanket to sit on.

* Stretch your legs out in front of you, and place your hands either side, palms down into the grass.

* Close your eyes and feel the refreshing energy of the meadow fill you up.

* Take a deep breath in, and, as you exhale, imagine the breath traveling down each arm, through the palm of each hand, and into the grass.

* Picture a carpet of beautiful flowers springing forth as your energy connects with the earth. See the blooms spread out, until they cover the entire meadow, field, or park.

* Continue to breathe in this way for a few minutes, keeping your focus on the breath, and the earth beneath you.

Guan Yin

Buddhist Goddess of Compassion and Mercy

THEMES
Compassion, empathy, kindness, abundance

"ONE WHO SEES AND HEARS THE CRIES OF THE WORLD"

A long time ago in China, there lived a woman so devoted to her faith and practice that it became her, and she became it. No longer governed by human concerns, there was no envy to her smile and no malice to her gestures. She wore her heart upon her sleeve, and gladly went about her service to others. Nothing was too much trouble, for she truly cared about the world around her.

She took the Buddhist teachings to her heart, practicing her mantras and meditations daily, but more than this, she had a deep understanding of all things spiritual, which she longed to pass on to others. While her friends and neighbors clambered to reach the top of their profession, or to outdo each other with their possessions, she realized that none of this mattered. To her, it was more important to be a good person, to care for each soul, and to live a simple life. So she did this, until the day she died.

But that is not her story's end—being so enlightened and having sacrificed so much during her journey upon the earth, she had earned the right to enter Nirvana. This was a great accolade, a blessing reserved for those who had showed love beyond measure. Nirvana is the highest state of wellbeing; a place where worldly suffering no longer exists and the soul is reborn into bliss. It is the ultimate goal on the Buddhist path, and a great honor.

As her soul floated before the light, ready to be extinguished of all pain, she heard the voice of the Buddha in her mind calling her forward.

"It is your time to reach the purest state of enlightenment. Come now. . . ." he urged her.

His words were like the petals of the lotus, soft and yielding, smooth and full of beauty, and she could feel

herself being drawn closer. Her spirit, light as a feather and imbued with brightness, drifted toward this heavenly vortex.

But then she heard something else, too, a sound that was barely there at first, but as she focused upon it, it became louder and louder. And she soon realized that it wasn't just one singular sound. It was many raised voices filled with anguish. She listened with every part of her being and heard the pain and suffering in their cries; there was a darkness that seemed to swallow everything, and she knew that she couldn't leave the world of the living behind. She deserved the peace of Nirvana, and yet the cries tugged at her heart, and filled her with so much sorrow that she stopped floating toward the ether, and instead reached out with what was left of her soul. She reached down from the cosmos, her arms open to all those who were struggling, and then she spoke.

"I cannot leave this way. I hear the cries of those suffering, and I long to help, to do what I can to alleviate their pain. This is my calling."

There was silence and a moment when it seemed the world stopped turning, for who had ever renounced eternal bliss, to return to a place of burden? Who, except Guan Yin, "she who observes the sounds," a being of great mercy and understanding.

Some people saw her as the "one with a thousand arms," for it is true that the needs of many were overwhelming, and as she tried to reach out to all the people who cried, her arms split into a thousand pieces. On seeing this, Buddha turned them into a thousand arms, giving her the power to soothe as many souls as possible.

Carrying her water vase in one hand and a willow branch in the other, she bestowed the nectar of life upon her followers, sprinkling it over them until they were filled with love. The willow she took as her symbol, to represent unbreakable strength, and the ability to be flexible in the face of adversity. She made it her mission to take away the pain.

From that moment, that is what she became; a deity for those in need. And while she did not reach Nirvana, she remained immortal in the hearts and minds of the people she cared for. She became Guan Yin, the goddess of mercy and compassion.

"I treat everyone I meet with compassion and empathy."

GODDESS RITUAL

Guan Yin is selfless. She puts the needs of others first, and cares so deeply that she feels their pain. Her empathic powers mean she can identify and connect with her followers, and in turn lift their spirits. She encourages us to connect with others in the same way.

This ritual works with the heart chakra to promote compassion and help us send loving energy to those who need it.

You will need a piece of rose quartz, a pillow or cushion, and somewhere comfortable to lay down where you won't be disturbed.

Lay down with your head upon the pillow, and position the rose quartz over your heart chakra, which is in the middle of your chest. This center governs the flow of energy from the heart. Rose quartz is a gentle stone, which promotes compassion and can help you open yourself up to others.

With your arms at your side, relax and take a deep breath in. As you do, imagine you're drawing in energy from the stone. See it as a rosy, pink light that seeps into your chest, flooding the space with warmth.

As you exhale, imagine you're sending out this loving energy and see it fill the space around you.

Take your time and repeat this cycle of breathing, visualizing the lovely pink energy filling you up as you inhale, and then filtering into the atmosphere as you exhale.

Spend at least five minutes practicing this breathing technique, then when you're ready, remove the stone and keep it with you as a reminder to be open-hearted and ready to connect with others.

Hathor

THEMES
Motherhood, fertility, gratitude, the arts

"A MOTHER'S LOVE"

As with any age and culture, there are always those who suffer and those who excel. And in ancient Egypt it was just as true as anywhere else. For while the rich sat upon their thrones adorned in finery, the poor walked the dusty streets barefoot, and paid lip-service to their idols; the deities they hoped would turn their fortunes around.

Most of the gods and goddesses had distinct roles, and as such would not get involved in anything outside their remit. After all, they could only do so much, and they were celestial beings, meaning they had a choice. They didn't have to help humankind if they didn't want to. Sometimes it was much more pleasing to simply let them work it out for themselves.

There was one exception; Hathor, the mother goddess. She was all things to all people and while some of the other pantheon sneered that she was mistress of all trades, and therefore hardly an expert at one, it didn't bother her.

Hathor loved her people, like a mother doting upon her children. She longed to bring them joy and sustenance and to provide for them in ways that the other gods wouldn't understand. She was, after all, the mother of the great sun god Ra, and expertly placed to watch over the earth, for every day she would ride with him through the sky. And like a mother, she worried for her children. She wanted them to be happy and tried to give them everything they needed. When the men in their dirty robes asked for abundance to make life a little easier, she would supply it. When the newlywed women asked to be blessed with fertility, it was her they called upon, and when, in the throes of labor, they cried out in agony, it was Hathor who mopped their brow and soothed them. When evil tainted

the earth, she would take it upon herself to drive it out, using the power of music. She'd parade through the streets playing her sistrum, and the very sound of the instrument and her dancing would inspire goodness. All these things she did willingly because that is what a mother does.

But like any mother of a thousand children, she could not be everywhere all at once. And there must have been some who wondered if she would ever answer their prayers. Perhaps that is why Hathor became the Queen of the Heavens, the mother of all the deities and associated with many of the other goddesses who took on an aspect of her role. For even the most powerful of them all needs a helping hand every now and then. Even the best mother in the world will have problems with her children.

Known as the Eye of Ra, and wearing her red solar disc above her head, Hathor had the power to destroy the world at her fingertips and could easily have struck down those ungrateful souls who did nothing but complain. Instead she reached out, this time in the guise of a white cow. She appeared to the gathered throng, who did nothing but grumble at their misfortunes, and, carrying a tray of food upon her head, she set it down before them. She stood silently as they ate, a beast of the field and nothing like the golden goddess of myth and legend, and her udders flowed with milk. Her people, for their part, could see that Hathor was truly loving and giving, and they acknowledged this by building temples in her name and celebrating her deeds.

Hathor was touched by their gratitude, and the more they thanked her, the more she repaid them with gifts and pleasures, and soon the people realized that to be truly grateful was the only way to experience real joy.

No longer was she one goddess, but she became the Seven Hathors, and present at the birth of every human to decide their fate. Some say she had the head of a cow, while others only the ears or horns. There were those who saw her as the beast in full, with skin as white as the moon, and those whose vision was of a woman surrounded by stars. So many forms and responsibilities did the great goddess have, but the most important one of all was that of mother. It is with a mother's love that Hathor became the mistress of heaven.

"I nurture myself and others, by showing care and gratitude."

GODDESS RITUAL

Hathor was a busy lady, having so many different responsibilities, but she made short work of it, and was only too happy to help. A nurturing goddess, she wanted the best for everyone, and in giving to others she gained great rewards herself. She shows us that in order to experience true joy and abundance, we must learn to share it with others.

This ritual, which focuses on helping others, will give you a sense of purpose and help you feel both nurtured and nurturing.

* You're going to create a nurture notebook, in which you can journal and brainstorm ideas that will help you feel nurtured and spread the love.

* You'll need a notebook that you like—you can invest in a special one, or go for something plain but then decorate the outer cover with pictures or quotes, for example.

* Start with yourself and make a list of things that make you feel nurtured, things like time in nature, meditation, exercise, and so on.

* Follow this by thinking about others and what you think would make them feel nurtured, things like a hug, cooking them a nice meal, sharing words of encouragement, and so on.

* Look at both lists and make a point of choosing one or two things from each list that you can do for yourself and others, as part of your weekly routine.

* Once you have done these things, be sure to write about your experiences in the notebook, consider how you felt, and any feedback from other people.

* Continue to work your way through the lists and add to them regularly. Also reflect upon your experiences and how they made you feel.

Idun

Norse Goddess of the Spring

THEMES
Rejuvenation, youthfulness, fertility, growth

"THE APPLES OF IMMORTALITY"

There was once a youthful goddess called Idun. Known as "the rejuvenator," she lived in the Norse land Asgard with her poet husband, Bragi, and together they would entertain the deities in the main hall. Her lightness of being and loveliness was often commented on, as she accompanied Bragi during his poetic retellings. She was so imbued with vitality that it was often asked, "How do you stay so young? What is your secret?" Questions to which she would respond with a coy smile, and a flutter of her eyelashes. It's true that Idun did have the secret to immortality, which she eventually shared with the other deities, although where she had found such a mystical treasure, no one knows.

Idun was the keeper of the apples of immortality—a fruit so ripe and sweet that just one bite would be enough to impart a youthful blessing. She carried the fruit in her small box made of ash, and while many didn't realize that this was where the true magic was hidden, it soon became obvious that Idun was desired for this gift. The apples, tinged with gold and gleaming like the sun, were all that was needed to keep the other gods happy. The minute they began to show any signs of aging they would call upon Idun, and she would give them an apple. Once consumed the fruit would work its enchantment, and any visible wrinkles would disappear, along with aches, pains, and other signs of old age.

While most were grateful for this gift, and for the joy that Idun brought them, some of the gods were less pleased. And so it was that the trickster god Loki found himself in some trouble with the giant Thjazi, who wanted to kill him. Loki struck a deal. He would help the giant steal Idun and her apples away from Asgard, in return for

his life. This was something that pleased Thjazi much, for he secretly coveted the goddess and her magical fruit.

"Sweet Idun," Loki said one day, "I know of a wood where there is a precious and rare fruit, to match your magical apples. Would you like me to show you the way?" The goddess was intrigued and agreed to go with Loki to see this treasure for herself. Little did she realize she was being lured away. When she arrived at the wood, she found Thjazi waiting in the form of a giant eagle. He swept her up in his claws, and away to his lofty realm in Jötunheimr.

This could have been the end of Idun, and her apples, but the rest of the deities were distraught. Slowly and surely, they began to age and, once the process had started, it picked up speed like a stone rolling downhill. From drooping jaws and a wobbly gait, to wrinkles that stole away their beauty, the gods began to lose their charm, with little they could do about it.

"Who was the last of us to see Idun?" they yelled, and the answer came back through the gathered throng, "Loki, it was Loki." They all knew of the trickster's deceitful and selfish ways, so they challenged him on the subject. After much persuasion he conceded that it was his fault she had disappeared and told them what he had done.

"I can get her back," he said. "Give me Freya's falcon feather cloak. I will fly to the realm of Jötunheimr and help her escape."

While the gods had little love for him, and trusted him even less, it was their only option for they were aging fast, and they had't the energy to rescue her themselves.

Once Loki donned Freya's feathery cloak he assumed the shape of a falcon and flew to Thjazi's hall. There he found the goddess on her own, weeping. Taking her hand, he transformed her into a nut, which he swiftly carried back to Asgard, and to the arms of the poet Bragi. In the meantime, the giant Thjazi got wind of his plans and followed him in his eagle form, but the gods were prepared and had built a great fire, with flames that stretched to the heavens. Quick-thinking Loki escaped the searing heat, but Thjazi was not so lucky and met his doom.

And so it was a happy end for the gods of the Aesir. Spring had returned and the restorative powers of Idun's apples transformed each deity into a vision of youthfulness. New shoots began to grow, and the earth was abundant with greenery. The gods blossomed, just like the fruit upon the tree, and the goddess Idun remained true to her name, "the young one," "the rejuvenator," and the "keeper of the apples of immortality."

"Finding a moment of joy every day rejuvenates my spirit."

GODDESS RITUAL

Idun is full of youthful promise and optimism. She offers us the chance to renew body and soul, and feel rejuvenated, through the power of nature and in doing the things we love.

This ritual, which works with the senses and the natural landscape, will help you feel rejuvenated and put a spring in your step!

You're going to take a mindful walk in your local park, countryside, or your yard. It doesn't matter how big or small the space is, you can still engage all your senses and reap the benefits.

* As you walk, or stand if you haven't much space, engage all your senses one by one.

* Start with what you see, and pick out something that stands out, like a beautiful flower. Examine it in detail and take in its shape and form.

* Identify all the different sounds that you can hear and how they come together to make a natural symphony. Enjoy listening to the composition.

* Take a deep breath in through your nose and follow each scent. What do you smell?

* Drink the air down deep into your belly. What do you taste?

* Finally, what can you feel? Perhaps it is raining, and you feel tiny pinpricks of water against your skin, or if it's sunny, notice where you feel the warmth the most.

* To finish, think of a word that sums up how you feel right now, and carry that feeling with you through the rest of your day.

Air, Sky, and the Winds of Change

Light as a feather, and weightless as air, the goddesses in this section cannot always be seen. Some are ethereal, and have a dreamlike quality, while others thunder their way into existence. They cut a path through the sky, and make their presence felt like a hearty gust of wind that knocks you sideways. These are the queens of the heavens, the harbingers of change, who can turn your life upside-down in a heartbeat, but that doesn't mean they should be feared. These deities will help you understand the unexpected nature of life, and also the gentle whisper of inspiration as it blows into your mind.

Some may have nothing to do with the sky, the stars, or the weather, but feature the element of air in another way. After all, air is oxygen. It's the fuel that feeds the mind and intellect, and quenches our imagination. It pushes us forward when we least expect it, bringing transformation and new beginnings.

If you want to change your fate, these deities are the ones to call on. They may twist and turn, but they are always present and, just like the air we breathe, they have the power to sustain us.

Nut

Egyptian Goddess of the Sky

THEMES
Rebirth, patience, flexibility, creativity

"WHEN EARTH MEETS SKY"

Take a moment, take a breath, and look up. See the vast beauty that is the sky above your head. Relax, and soften your gaze. Notice how still and serene she seems, and yet there is movement, a gradual fading of color.

Clouds float by, stealing time and your imagination. Nothing stops; it is merely an illusion, a trick that she has perfected over millions of years. She hangs there, her slender form arched over the arc of the world. Her fingertips and toes brush the curve of the earth, longing to fall into the solid arms of her one true love, but she is enduring and clever. She does not complain. After all, this is who and what she is.

When the world first began, and there was little but a thought, a spark of an idea sitting at the heart of the universe, the goddess Nut was born. Daughter of the great god of air, Shu, and his loving wife Tefnut, goddess of heat and moisture, her destiny was set in motion. From her first breath it was expected that she would take her place, an endless and giving being who would form the heavens, while her brother Geb would become the earth at her feet.

A dutiful soul, whose one intention was to give back, she was made for this role. Day and night she curled above her brother the earth, protecting, strengthening, and watching over him as he grew in strength and power. She admired him greatly, and that soon evolved into a love that consumed her heart, for how could she not feel something? She spent every minute of every day gazing into his eyes and, as with so many of her kin, their relationship changed and her brother became her husband, and they were inseparable.

They clung together, merging heaven and earth to become one, but their blossoming love only served to anger Shu. This was not his intention, and in his rage, he flew between them, casting the goddess Nut aside, arms and legs stretched as he prized them apart.

"You were not meant for each other; this is not the order of things!" he cried, and in his fury, air spilled from his mouth and filled the space between them. It pushed the sky farther and farther away from the land, till she could only look from a distance through streaks of cloud and sunlight, and see what might have been.

For his part, Geb was heartbroken. How could he live without his glorious wife at his side, and yet there was nothing he could do. Already life was stirring, and in the heavenly womb of Nut, too, there was an awakening. Their union had produced a litter of stars and planets that would light up the sky, keeping her company on the darkest of days.

But Nut had a secret. She had a plan, for she knew over time her father Shu would waver, and the air between them would be charged with passion once more. And so each day, starting at dawn, she moved slowly, gently, in a graceful dance toward the earth. So cautious and light of foot

was she that nobody noticed. They did not see the sun begin to fade, or the shadow of night descend. They did not sense the heavy blanket laid upon them, until it was too late. By then sweet Nut had met her love once more, and they would be together, if only for a short while.

In that time, her children the stars and the moon would illuminate the sky and watch over the world, allowing her some respite. Then, just as slowly as before, she would crawl into position and cradle the earth below, while the air was none the wiser and a new day began. Such is the cycle of day and night, of earth and sky, of Geb and Nut, and so it goes on and their love is reborn, like the sun and the moon.

So take this moment to look up and see if you can catch her out. I guarantee, however hard you stare; however much you look into the air, you will never see her move. She might flicker and sway, and she will probably take your breath away with her beauty, but you won't see her coming. Before you know it, night will be upon you and Nut will be in the arms of Geb, and that is how it was meant to be since the world began.

"I bend, I breathe, I relax."

GODDESS RITUAL

Nut is patient. She knows there is a time for everything, and that with every ending there is a new beginning, a new day from which you can create great things. The cycles of life cannot be ignored and while we might feel like we're flying high one day, the next can bring us down to earth.

This ritual, which works with the element of air and simple movements, will help you go with the flow and develop patience and flexibility as you navigate the highs and lows. If you can, perform this ritual outside, looking up at the sky.

★ Position your feet hip-width apart, roll your shoulders back, tilt your chin upward, and lengthen your spine.

★ Take a long, deep breath in. Draw the air into your chest and, as you exhale, raise your arms above your head.

★ As you move, feel the air wrap around you. Notice how it supports each movement that you make.

★ Next, lunge forward with your right leg, bending at the knee. Inhale, and, as you exhale, sweep your arms down.

★ Again, notice how the air feels against your skin, and how it works with you to accentuate each stretch.

★ Bring your left leg level with your right and bounce lightly. Take another deep breath in and straighten your legs.

★ As you exhale, begin to twist from your waist, first right and then left. Let your arms hang loose and continue to breathe deeply.

★ Enjoy the flexibility as your joints and limbs sweep through the air.

★ To finish, say, "I move with ease and go with the flow."

Juno

THEMES
Honesty, loyalty, truth,
inner strength

**"HOW THE PEACOCK GOT
ITS TAIL FEATHERS"**

There was once a mother goddess, a divine being in the Roman pantheon who was loved by all, except her husband, the god Jupiter. Her name was Juno, and she was the "bringer of light," the mother of all, and a champion of women. Not one to be trifled with, she was known for her strength, and her jealousy, although when it came to her people she had a generous heart, and gave freely of her time and energy. She helped the poor and needy, and to them she was Juno Sospita, the savior of humankind. She assisted in financial matters, and in this guise she was Juno Moneta, and as head of the state and Queen of the Heavens, she was Juno Regina.

But the role that caused her the most pain was Juno, the wife of Jupiter, for he was a fickle god, governed by lusty whims. Even so, Juno took her marriage seriously, and because of this was often called upon to bless marital affairs and help young brides conceive.

While she put a brave face on when helping her people, deep down she was in constant turmoil, for it was hard to continue with such grace and virtue when her own husband showed her little respect. She would sit on her plinth among the stars, a moon goddess governed by the waters beneath her, and her emotions would shift and change with the tides.

Juno knew that to be true to herself, she would have to be courageous and deliver judgment upon Jupiter and his conquests. And as hard as this was, because she deeply loved the god, she would have to rise up and stand her ground. She was, after all, a strong and mighty woman, and her actions defined her, so she spent much of her time trying to catch him out.

While he had many liaisons, one of the most prominent was his affair with the priestess Io. Initially she spurned his advances, but Jupiter was persistent in his ardor, and eventually the two embarked upon a romance. When Juno discovered the deception, she was mortified and determined to make both the god and the priestess pay—but Jupiter was powerful and had his spies, and so to protect his lover he turned her into a heifer.

On learning of Io's transformation, Juno enlisted the help of Argus, a hideous monster with 100 eyes. She asked him to use his enhanced vision to keep watch over Io. She wanted to know where she was at any given time, and to keep track on any lovers' trysts. She had a soft spot for the creature, and knew that he would be only too happy to help for he was a loyal servant. Little did she realize she was sending him to his doom, for clever Jupiter always seemed to be one step ahead. He sent the god Mercury to put an end to the beast, which he did by lulling him to sleep, then slaughtering him where he lay.

Juno was devastated. Above all else, she had a big heart and felt responsible for his death. Being the "bringer of light" she had to turn the situation around, to do something to commemorate his faithfulness. As she looked at his broken body, and lifeless eyes, she couldn't help but notice their beauty. It was then that she had an idea.

Kneeling before him, she placed a hand upon his head and whispered these words; "My loyal Argus, in life they called you a monster, but in death I will transform you into something exquisite as a reward for all you have done for me!"

Carefully, so as not to destroy their vivid color, she gathered up the monster's 100 eyes. Then, summoning her power, she cast them out into the ether while making a silent wish that they should take their rightful place in the world. So it was that the eyes found their way into the tail feathers of the peacock, a bird most revered at that time. There they settled among the finery and every time the bird chose to display its magnificence, the eyes appeared, staring out from the splayed plumes—a reminder of Argus and a symbol of power and sovereignty.

Juno continued to rule, and dominate the minds of the Roman people, despite her husband's dalliances. She became known for her inner strength, and her ability to stand up for the truth at all costs.

"Being honest with myself and others is the key to my inner strength."

GODDESS RITUAL

Juno was a well-loved mother goddess. She was considered kind, truthful, and just in all things. While she was depicted as a strong and mighty adversary, her courage was a result of her self-belief and her honorable actions. She didn't shy away from the truth, even if it was uncomfortable.

This ritual, which uses a feather, a symbol associated with this goddess, will help to cleanse your aura and clear away fear and doubt, so that you, too, can act with courage and honor.

You will need a large feather—any type will do—it doesn't have to be a peacock feather. The idea is that you are tapping into the symbolism of this bird.

✴ Take the feather and, starting at the top of your head, briskly flick it outward, as if flicking away dust and debris.

✴ Work your way around the body, going down each side, under each foot, and around to the other side.

✴ As you flick, imagine you are cleaning your aura, the energy field around your body. The brisk action of the feather gets any stagnant energy moving and eliminates negativity.

✴ Breathe deeply as you do this and, when you've finished, take a couple of long breaths to ground yourself.

✴ Say, "I am cleansed, renewed, and ready to take a stand. My aura is imbued with courage."

Bixia Yuanjin

TAOIST GODDESS OF THE WIND, DAWN, AND DESTINY

THEMES
Inspiration, imagination, liberation, manifestation

"PRINCESS OF THE ROSY CLOUDS"

When a child is born, there is a celestial celebration. The gods and goddesses come together and smile down upon the tiny soul before them. They gather in a heavenly host, like proud godparents, and take in the beauty of the babe as it takes its first breath, and it is a moment of pure joy. But the most important of all the deities is the sweet goddess of the dawn, Bixia Yuanjin. For when she casts a loving glance in their direction, she dictates the future. Being born of cloud and stardust, she is the one who has the power to determine destiny and inspire the child's path. It is a fitting task for a goddess who appears at the beginning of each new day. She stands at the brow of the hill, and lets her fingers do a delicate dance through the air, so the first breath of wind rises and the morning comes.

She is the princess of the rosy clouds, a wind goddess who has built a castle in the sky from which to look down upon her people. And in return she urges them to look up, to climb to the highest point and breathe deep of the air, for in doing so, they take the goddess to their soul. While many of the deities believe in their own self-importance and perform supernatural feats to prove their worth, Bixia Yuanjin does not have to. Her powers are clear to see every day. For while fire and flood strike terror in the hearts of any human, and can be seen as punishments from above, they do not inspire change.

When the gods of the Taoist realm couldn't decide who should have the honor of predetermining fate from birth, they put on a display of their powers, a heavenly contest so that the mightiest of them all could emerge.

As you can imagine, such a performance set the skies alight, as each deity took center stage in a bid to be the best

of all. The rain gods drew deep from the wells of water within their bellies, and it poured and poured. Great rivers cascaded over the land. The streams merged into lakes, lakes into oceans, and still the water came; it was a tremendous sight. Then it was the turn of the thunder gods. With their silvery whips and swords they sliced through the air, cutting the sky in two and delivering bolts that made the earth shudder. The heavens were alive with color and light, and the show that followed was spectacular. Then came the sun gods; all brightness and passion, they turned up the heat on their fiery orbs, sending rays of burning light in every direction. They smashed through the darkness and made all the excess water disappear. Still they fizzled and raged, the land began to harden and crack, and the burnished amber of the sky was breathtaking.

However, it was only Bixia Yuanjin who asked the most important question, the one that made all the gods stop and think.

"What about the humans?" she said. "Yes, you put on great displays of power, but what about them? They suffer at your hands, and you do nothing to lift them up." And in that moment, she descended from her cloud castle in the sky and began

to blow a soothing breeze upon the land. The air became cool and fresh, the burned orange vista turned rosy pink, and the humans below looked up. They could feel the wind urging them to climb higher, to gulp down the fresh air and clear their lungs of dust and debris. So they began to climb, to clamber up the mountains, and though it was arduous, they were determined to reach the top. When they did, they opened their arms wide to embrace the sweet air. Drinking down long, deep breaths, their minds were cleared and their bodies energized. They suddenly felt inspired, and propelled to do great things with their lives.

It was then that the deities agreed that while they were all mighty, it was Bixia Yuanjin who had the power to shape human souls. She was the one who had come to their aid, who had filled them with lifegiving breath. She was the one who had triggered their imaginations and encouraged them to climb higher than ever before. She was the princess of the rosy clouds, Queen of the Dawn, and the bringer of liberation.

"With every breath, I climb higher to reach my goals!"

GODDESS RITUAL

Bixia Yuanjin uses her powers to lift people up. She is the sweet wind of inspiration and the vibrant, forceful wind of change. When she sweeps through the world she clears a path, so that new things can be born, in the shape of ideas, emotions, and adventures. She can help you manifest the future and attract new opportunities.

This ritual, which taps into the element of air, will help to uplift your body and mind, and promote new ideas.

You will need to find a hill or mountain to climb. This doesn't have to be a mammoth task—a small incline is enough—but it helps if you are in an exposed space that is slightly higher than normal.

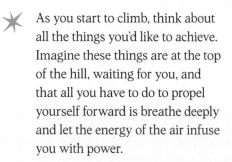

As you start to climb, think about all the things you'd like to achieve. Imagine these things are at the top of the hill, waiting for you, and that all you have to do to propel yourself forward is breathe deeply and let the energy of the air infuse you with power.

Focus on your breath as you take each step, and extend the length of each gulp of air. You should notice that you feel more energized and positive the higher you climb.

When you reach the top, stand for a moment and drink in the space.

Notice any breeze, and how it feels against your skin.

Welcome it into your life by throwing your arms open and spinning around.

Say out loud or in your head, "Let the wind breathe new life and energy into my dreams."

Iris

Greek Goddess of the Rainbow

THEMES
Communication, hope, joy, service

"AFTER THE RAIN"

When the earth was still in its fledgling state, and its people were beginning to strike out on their own, there was much consternation among the pantheon of Greek deities. They watched from their ornately adorned palaces in the sky, they peered into the lives of the lost and lovelorn, and absorbed their stories for entertainment, and yet there was little they could do to influence events. They were merely heavenly spectators, and as such would remain impartial, unless they were called upon specifically to help. Even then they were limited in what they could do. There are, after all, certain rules to be followed, as with all things.

A deity could be petitioned with the right choice of words and worship. Offerings laid at the altar or shrine were a sure way to get their attention, but sometimes even then, they were of the wrong kind. The differences between gods and men have caused many great battles and, in some ways, it's easy to see why. Men are mortal; they don't have the luxury of eternity to make mistakes and learn from them. Time moves fast, and nothing stays the same, but for the deities there is little change, little to amuse them, except the daily doings of their people.

And so it was that the gods and goddesses decided there should be a go-between, a messenger who could straddle both worlds with ease. As you can imagine this role was treated with much respect, and well sought after. It was unique, which meant that all the better-known deities wanted it for themselves. The chance to make a real connection, to be involved in the comings and goings of humankind, was a dream come true, and arguments soon followed.

"It should be me; I am the oldest."

"No, it should be me! I am the most powerful."

"You're both wrong, it should be me, I am the wisest of you all!"

And so it went on. . . .The heavens were full of fury, and it seemed that nothing could soothe the situation, until out of a flurry of clouds and with the lightest of steps came a girl, daughter of the marine god Thaumas and his nymph bride, Elektra. With delicate features and a voice that sang through the air, she passed between them all, unseen, leaving ribbons of color in her wake. In her hands she held a jug filled with the sweetest nectar, which she served dutifully to the great god and father of them all, Zeus.

As she did so, a hush fell on the crowd. In that moment they all understood that this lesser-known goddess was the only one with the attributes needed to be the perfect messenger. Being fleet of foot, and gentle in her ways, she could move swiftly between the heavenly and earthly realms. This, coupled with her keenness to serve, and her honesty, meant there would be no need for confusion, no ulterior motives or power games. This was a goddess whose aura glowed with hope and promise.

And so sweet Iris was proclaimed the messenger god, the one who would travel between worlds to deliver insights, information, and help. But the next question was, how? To come with a crack of thunder, breaking through the clouds would not do, for it would surely scare the humans. To arrive in a flurry of bells and horns, upon a chariot or winged steed was also too much, so how would the people know that she was on her way? What sign would alert them to her presence?

Again, Iris answered the question. As she flexed her golden wings and sailed through the air, her multicolored ribbons stretched before her in a perfect arc. The arch this created seemed to skim the surface of the ocean, and extend all the way up to the stars, making a beautiful rainbow of light. Those who saw it would gasp in wonder and read it as sign that something good was on its way.

The deities beamed at their own magnificence, to come up with such a solution! How powerful and mighty they must appear to humankind. Little did they realize that the answer had been there all along, and that the people of the earth have always known that after the rain, comes hope in the guise of a rainbow.

"Every step I take imbues me with hope."

GODDESS RITUAL

Iris is known as a cup bearer and spent most of her time replenishing the rain clouds with water from the sea. A generous and helpful deity, she moved between realms as a messenger between the humans and the gods, keeping the channels of communication open and spreading light and love.

This ritual generates positive energy, which helps to improve the way you think and feel, and attracts more of the same, making you a conduit of light and a joy to be around!

This exercise is best performed in the morning, to give you a positive mindset for the day ahead.

✳ Stand in the shower and close your eyes. Breathe deeply to clear and calm your mind.

✳ Turn the shower on and spend a few minutes acclimatizing yourself to the temperature of the water.

✳ Imagine that the spray is infused with rainbow light, which cascades down and covers you in an array of colors.

✳ Notice the way the water hits the top of your head, and imagine that with every breath in, you draw this energy down through your spine.

✳ Feel the hues seep through your skin in rays of brightness that extend outward.

✳ Absorb this vibrant energy, and picture yourself wearing a rainbow-colored cloak.

✳ To finish, turn the temperature down for thirty seconds. Take a deep breath in and, as you exhale, feel the rainbow of light getting bolder and brighter.

✳ Throughout the day, bring the image of the rainbow cloak to mind. Imagine the colors extending outward, so that everyone you meet is bathed in the glow.

Minerva

Roman Goddess of Wisdom, Justice, and Victory

THEMES
Wisdom, philosophy, objectivity, integrity

"THE WEB WE WEAVE"

The deities of ancient Rome were not necessarily known for their intelligence. They tended to be governed by their desires, whether swayed by romantic gestures and lusty liaisons, like Venus, or driven half mad with power and a thirst for battle, like Mars. But there is always one whose narrative is different, a goddess with a combination of wit, wisdom, and good humor, and in this case, at this time, it was Minerva. Part of the eternal and supreme triad, along with Jupiter and Juno, this power threesome governed the land and weaved the fates, and Minerva was at the heart of the action.

That's not to say that she didn't have her weaknesses; being so accomplished in matters of finance, industry, and battle meant she was used to being top of the tree. Should anyone dare challenge her position or her abilities, then they would surely feel the force of Minerva's wrath. That said, her innate knowledge and understanding of people meant that unlike the other gods, she approached them with more humanity.

An adept warrior and clever to the point of cunning, it was hard to best her. Many humans tried, but only one really got under her skin. Beautiful and gifted, Arachne was a talented and confident weaver, but while she had great skill, she had little tact.

"I am the best weaver in the world. Why, I am surely better than Minerva herself!" she claimed, loud and often, and as with most claims that dare to mention the gods, their words are easily carried to heavenly ears. And so it was that Minerva heard the girl's boasts and decided to teach her a lesson.

With a flick of her fingers, she transformed from her usual ceremonial gown and helmet into the guise of an old

crone. Her fingers were wizened and worn to the bone, and her voice was a whisper.

"I hear you claim to be the best weaver," she said to the girl. "If that is the case, then I would like to challenge you to a wager." Arachne grinned. "I accept your challenge, for I know I will win!"

"Then let the contest begin," said Minerva, stabbing the air with a bent finger. "We shall each weave a tapestry in honor of the gods, then we'll see who is truly the best." They both worked into the night, deftly and swiftly, using intricate patterns and the brightest of thread, under the watchful eye of the deities. Minerva was nothing if not fair and insisted that no trickery would be used to win her claim.

At the end they each presented their tapestry. Minerva went first with her wonderous creation of the patronage of Athens, and while it was skillfully woven, and breathtaking in size, it paled at the side of Arachne's vision. She too had paid tribute to the god's exploits, and the weaving did indeed excel Minerva's in its detail and flair—but she had showed the gods engaging in folly, seducing human women and revealing their weaknesses.

Minerva, having shifted form from crone to goddess, could feel the rumblings up above. She knew that the gods were enraged by what they saw, for how could a human poke such fun at them? Acting quickly, she struck the girl in the face. Arachne was deeply humiliated. To be chastised by the goddess Minerva was to be shamed in a public way.

Taking a length of rope, she strung it through the rafters and made a noose for her neck, then hung herself. While the deities cackled and jeered, Minerva felt nothing but pity. She had only meant to teach the girl a lesson. Her death would not be justice, it would be futile, and the goddess had the good sense to know this, so with another flick of her fingers she performed some magic.

She sprinkled some of the goddess Hecate's herb, otherwise known as rue, upon the girl, and in an instant her hair fell out. Her gowns crumpled to the floor as her human body was transformed into something small and round and black that scuttled across the stones. Her slender fingers became spindly legs attached to a hairy body from which she would spin her silvery thread. And then Minerva spoke, and all the ears of the world and the heavenly realm listened.

"Little spider, sweet arachnid—the web we weave determines our fate, and this is yours. Spin it well and know that you *are*, and always will be, the best weaver in the world."

"My intuition infuses every thought, word, and deed."

GODDESS RITUAL

Minerva was clever and liked to take a step back and see both sides of the situation. Her objectivity meant she had all the information and was able to form judgments based on what she saw and felt inside. This ritual, which uses the spider's web as its focus, will help you plan and problem solve.

You will need a large piece of paper and some pens.

★ If you have a problem or decision to make, summarize the details in one or two words.

★ On the paper, write the words in the center, then draw a circle around them.

★ Consider what you could do to move away from this. Perhaps there's an action you can take, for example, doing some research on similar situations.

★ Draw a line from the circle and draw another circle. Write a few words inside to summarize this action. Spend some time thinking of other actions you can take and draw more lines and circles extending from the central circle.

★ Take each separate action/circle and consider what you might need to make this work. For example, if you said you'd need to do some research, where could you do this? On the internet? At a library? Talking to experts or a mentor?

★ Continue to draw more lines and circles for each one, and then do this for all the actions you originally listed.

★ By the time you've finished you should have something that resembles a spider's web, with lots of ideas that you can take inspiration from.

★ Use this as a starting point to take action and help you in the future.

Oya

Yoruban Goddess of Thunder, Lightning, and Storms

THEMES
Change, rebirth, justice, power

"SHE WHO TORE"

There was once a goddess who didn't know her own power. Born from the mother of the sea, she held all the elements within her grasp. In her veins the fresh water of the River Niger ran deep. In her hands the spark of fire sizzled. Above her head, the wind whipped nine tornadoes into a great frenzy, and in her heart she carried the dirt of the earth, the bone dust of the dead.

Beautiful and deadly, she was all things to all people, and perhaps in those early days she didn't recognize her own strength. After all, there are many who are gifted but fail to understand the truth of their talents. For Oya it was probably this way. The sister wife to her brother Shango, the legendary ruler of the fourth kingdom Oyo, in the beginning she lived in his shadow, not realizing that she, too, had great strength at her fingertips.

When the change came, it was as much of a surprise to her as it was to those who witnessed it. There was a rage within this goddess, a force that came bubbling forth when she was faced with deceit of any kind, and as humans we are never blameless. We have the capacity to take things for granted, again and again.

Oya watched from her place in the clouds. She made it her mission to read the minds of men and protect her people. To provide rain when it was needed and psychic insights when they were petitioned. To champion women, watch over them during childbirth, and lead the souls of the dead to their final resting place. All of this she did selflessly. The waters of the Niger were her gift to quench the spirits of her beloved people and cleanse them of their sins, but they could also be her curse.

In the early days, Oya loved deeply, and she shared that love freely, but then humankind became greedy,

and needy. Envy took hold and turned to jealousy, and people who had once been friends turned their backs on each other. They lied and cheated to work their way to the top, without considering others. They became self-centered. Families that had once shared bread with their neighbors, shut their doors. Villagers who had been only too happy to reach out and help a brother in need, closed themselves off. We became I, and I came first, and that made Oya angry.

Blood red, the anger boiled, it seethed within, and it seethed without, staining her robes a deep scarlet. The spark she held within her hands began to itch, and the winds that were only a whisper in her head grew in ferocity. The earth began to shudder as the dead stirred, but still the humans carried on, so consumed in their own mire they didn't realize that something was awakening.

The sky blackened and became thick and cloying, the air split in two and there at the center stood Oya, sword in hand. Below, the people stared yet failed to see why she was so enraged. What could they have possibly done to bring about such wrath? Blinded by their own importance, it was clear that change was needed.

Raising her silver sword above her head, she sliced through the clouds, sending a shaft of lightning down to earth. The bolt hit, smashing through roofs, sending sparks of fire in every direction. Oya watched with glee as huts and houses crumbled. She threw her hands in the air in disbelief and sent her nine whirlwinds tumbling across the land. She roared with laughter as the earth cracked open, and the people fell within, and when she could scream no more, when all the devastation had been wreaked, she walked away.

But that is not the end of the story. The people wept, and they wept. They shook in terror, and they broke their hearts. They reached out to each other, and shared in the grief, and all of this Oya witnessed from her throne in the sky. She looked on as they clung together, and she saw what she had done. While most deities would have turned away (after all, it was their misdeeds that had led to their undoing), Oya's heart broke too. It split in two then shattered, and the tears began to fall in great rivers. The heavens opened once more, and the rain came down. It poured through the streets, sweeping away all the debris. It washed away the blood and cleansed the upturned faces. It quenched the spirit of those who were dying and awakened those who had already passed.

In that moment, everything was made clean and the goddess who had not known her own power stepped into it, fully and totally. She made everything right once more and became Oya, "She who tore," and "The Great Mother of the Elders of the Night."

GODDESS AFFIRMATION

"I step into my personal power; I am the champion of me."

GODDESS RITUAL

Passionate Oya will do anything to protect her people, but should they betray her trust, then she isn't afraid to express herself. Considered a bringer of change, Oya is all about girl power and can help you embrace the unexpected and transform your world.

This ritual boosts personal power and helps to turn up your shine by encompassing Oya's symbol, the sword, and the element of fire.

You will need a penknife to represent Oya's sword, a pen and paper, and a red candle.

- To start, spend a few moments in quiet reflection and think about when you felt at your most powerful. Imagine you're stepping back to that time, and relive those emotions.

- Now take a minute to think about a symbol that represents that feeling, for example, you might choose the sun, as it's synonymous with joy and power. If you prefer you can think of a word, but choose something simple. Write this down in front of you.

- Now take your knife, or a pin if you prefer, and have a go carving the symbol or word into the wax of the candle.

- Light the candle and spend a few minutes gazing at the flame. Notice how it gets bigger and brighter with every breath you take.

- Focus on the symbol or word and know that whenever you need to step into your power, you can bring this to mind.

Melissa

Greek Bee Goddess

THEMES
Intuition, divine feminine power, kindness

"NECTAR OF THE GODS"

She so small and round, with her translucent wings and constant buzzing sound, a girl-like nymph, a goddess, a bee. Melissa, they called her, and she was all three. "It's no wonder she frightened gods and men alike. For she was a curious sight for a nymph, a curious sight for any kind of being!

She lived in a cave high on Mount Ida in Crete. Perhaps she hid away, for fear that people would see her, or hear the thrumming sound that her wings made as they flapped. It would explain her domain, for a cave is a strange place to find any kind of nymph. But Melissa, as she was known, was no ordinary being. There was magic in everything she did, from the delicate touch of her fingertips to her large shining eyes, and the way she moved. And perhaps no one would have discovered her existence if it hadn't been for Zeus.

He was just a tiny baby at the time, long before he became the great god that we are familiar with. This was before his time on Mount Olympus and all his many exploits. In this guise he was young and helpless, and would surely have died had it not been for the goat's milk that nourished him, and one other thing—the sweet, golden honey that Melissa placed upon his lips. She did this gently, using the tip of her finger, scooping up the mixture and feeding him, bit by bit, and watching in delight as he cooed and lapped it up.

And perhaps that is why he grew to be so big and strong, and why his powers flourished more than all the other gods. Perhaps it was the honey that imbued him with supernatural strength and a steely might. Or maybe it was Melissa herself who was the real key to his magic. For it cannot be denied that she knew the secrets

of the bees, and how to find and make the substance that would eventually become known as the "nectar of the gods." She had the power of transformation within her and, like an alchemist, could change one thing to another and produce something new and powerful. This would surely have influenced a young Zeus and shaped his impressionable mind.

She so small and round, and with her translucent wings, might have appeared odd upon first glance, but her gift to Zeus was not forgotten, whatever role it played in his rise to fame. As he grew and became the father of the gods, he realized that he owed this kindly nymph a great debt.

Her strange appearance did not matter. It was her loving, giving nature that he would acknowledge, and so in time Melissa became Queen Bee and a goddess in her own right. She had her temple of worship and many priestesses, too. These gifted accomplices, called the Melissae, also learned the way of the bee and followed in her footsteps. They sang her praises and performed ritualistic dances in honor of the nymph. They raised their voices, to create a buzzing throng because they

recognized her power and worth, and they, too, were worshipped and called upon for their honey-making skills. They danced the waggle dance of the bees, and walked their honeycomb path, and must have been quite a sight to the people of ancient Greece who knew little of beekeeping at that time. Not only that, but they were also acknowledged for their prophetic powers, and sought out for visions and predictions of the future.

The nectar of the gods was soon in demand. It was much revered, and used in food and drink to nourish and heal the bodies of those who were ailing. This magical cure-all from the goddess was more powerful than any other drug. It helped to bind wounds and soothe those who were suffering.

And who'd have thought it, coming from one so curious in shape and design? But greatness takes many forms and is often missed upon first glance.

"She so small and round, with her translucent wings and constant buzzing sound, a girl-like nymph, a goddess, a bee. Melissa, they called her, and she was all three."

"I embrace the divine feminine power within me."

GODDESS RITUAL

Melissa is a nurturing goddess. She gives freely of her magical gifts. She is happy to share and show others how to find the nectar of life. Irrespective of her appearance, her divine feminine energy is abundant, and people respect her for this. Melissa can show you how to step into your power and share your own gifts with the rest of the world.

This ritual, which uses Melissa's gift, honey, will help you acknowledge the divine feminine energy within, and unleash your unique beauty and power.

- Run a warm bath.

- Take a spoonful of honey and add it to half a glass of warm milk.

- Stir the honey into the milk and, as you do this, think about where this golden gift comes from.

- Once you've run your bath, pour in the milk and honey mixture, and swirl this around with your hand.

- Climb into the bath, and soak.

- Close your eyes, and imagine you're nestled in a golden hexagon of light. The divine feminine energy of the bee is at the heart of where you lay and is seeping into your body as you relax.

- When you breathe in, imagine you're breathing in golden light.

- As you breathe out, imagine you're releasing any negative energy. Feel your feminine power grow with every breath.

- To finish, say, "I unleash my natural beauty and let my divine feminine energy shine."

Ma'at

Egyptian Goddess of Justice

THEMES
Fairness, truth, justice, harmony

"THAT WHICH IS STRAIGHT AND TRUE"

No one knows how time began, how it came into being and started moving forward in a never-ending dance that would create new life, or how the world settled into its gentle rhythm, how things were set into being. But for the ancient Egyptians there was an order to everything, from the sun rising and setting, to the changing of the seasons and the course of the stars. Nothing was by chance, because chance was born from chaos, and the world would cease to exist without some kind of cosmic organization.

And so it was that Ma'at, the great winged goddess of justice, took her place in the pantheon of gods, at the foot of Ra. For when the sun god rose out of chaos, a stone mound came forth and it was there that she was formed. A being made of light and goodness, she was greatness personified and a representation of all that was fair and true in the world. Upon her head she wore an ostrich feather, protruding from a crown of gold. About her shoulders were wings to lift her high above the dusty streets, so high into the heavens that she would be able to see everything and oversee agreements and oaths as they were made.

Her role was to create order out of confusion, to see beyond the veil and judge the deeds of her people, when the time came for them to pass into the afterlife. It was an honor and a great responsibility, for she and only she could provide balance and structure.

And so being a dutiful deity, she took her place at the gates of the Underworld, ready to accept or reject the souls of the dead. But how would she come to such a conclusion fairly? Ma'at was all about fairness, and for her to bring judgment she would need structure, ritual, and a result

that could not be tainted by the hands of mortals or gods.

Standing at the dawn of time, with the power of the universe at her fingertips, and honesty flowing through her veins, Ma'at pondered her fate and the future of the world. Raising her hands to the heavens, she let her voice carry upward.

"That which is straight and true, I must divine. But how—with my head, with my heart, or something else of mine?" As the air shifted around her, and the feather above her head bristled, the answer came to her, as lightly and deeply as the first breath of life. It had been obvious all along; she had been given everything she needed to ascertain the truth.

"I will weigh the hearts of the dead upon the scales of balance and justice. I will place my ostrich feather on one side, and the heart on the other, and the truth will be revealed." She paused.

"And so it will be that if the heart is heavier than my feather, it is because it is weighed down with evil deeds and doings from a life that has been of little good. That soul will be judged, and the heart will be sent to the lake of fire where it will burn to cinders. If the heart is lighter or the same as my feather, then that is because the person did many good things while they walked the earth. That soul will be deemed

fit for the eternal afterlife and allowed entrance into that realm."

As she spoke, time moved and everything fell into place, and the people of ancient Egypt understood what was expected of them. They knew that they would eventually face the goddess Ma'at, and that she would judge them.

And this became the order of things. When a person passed into the valley of the dead, they would be met and taken to the Hall of Ma'at. She would greet them impassively and the ceremony would begin, and there could be no swaying from the rules, and no exceptions.

In this way, harmony would always reign. The people would know their place, and always seek the light, and Ma'at for her part would be known as "that which is straight and true," and honored for her role in life and death.

"I treat others, and myself, with respect and honesty."

GODDESS RITUAL

Ma'at was a physical manifestation of order and fairness, a symbol of honesty and truth; she would be present during times of discord, and to help her people make the right decisions. She could be counted on to weigh up the pros and cons and reveal the path of truth. In the same way, she can help you make decisions, and be true to yourself.

This ritual uses one of Ma'at's symbols, the scales of balance and judgment, to help you make decisions intuitively, and from a place of truth and honor.

You will need two small pieces of paper of roughly the same size, and a pen.

* If you are making a decision between two paths or choices, write one word on each piece of paper to represent each choice. For example, maybe you don't know whether to move to a new house, or stay where you are, so you might write "move" and "stay."

* Screw up the pieces of paper, then place one in each hand and form a fist.

* Hold both arms out in front of you at a level height. Keep your elbows relaxed and fists at the same height. You are creating the scales of Ma'at, using your body as a tool.

* Close your eyes and take a few deep, calming breaths.

* Ask the question, "Which choice is right for me, right now?"

* Relax and bring your attention to both hands. Does one feel heavier than the other? Perhaps one hand is dipping lower, or suddenly feels weightier. Maybe one hand is rising higher.

* Take note of what you feel; for example, one arm may begin to ache while the other doesn't.

* You'll know instinctively which choice is weighing heavy and which one feels lighter, and the right one for you.

Asteria

THEMES
Knowledge, enlightenment,
divination, clarity

"THE STARRY ONE"

There was once a goddess whose beauty shone so bright that it was rivalled only by the stars in the sky. On seeing her face, gods and mortals alike would fall at her feet, for she was truly breathtaking, from the curls in her hair to the starry shimmer of her eyes, and when she smiled it was like the brightest comet in the night sky. Around her head she wore a halo of stars, and this only enhanced her charms, for when you gazed up into the sky it would draw your attention, leaving you spellbound.

Her name was Asteria, the starry one, born to the Titans Phoebe and Coeus, children of the great god Uranus. She would take her place in the heavens as one of the earliest in the Greek pantheon, and while all the other gods played with the lives of humankind, causing chaos and strife, Asteria simply sat with her constellations admiring the view. She soon realized that there was power in the night sky, and that while she did not intervene in life upon earth, she could still pull some strings with the stars.

She would admire the shape and form of each constellation and make pictures in her head using the patterns. A gifted storyteller, it was easy to create narratives that held meaning, and so Asteria became adept at astrology, and the astrological influence of the planets upon the earth. This to her was far more powerful than throwing thunderbolts or magical love arrows, for it was predetermined, and could change a person's fate.

And so the sky became Asteria's playground, and she danced through the heavens leaving a trail of shooting stars in her wake. As you might imagine, she attracted a lot of attention. Her stunning appearance, along with a star-studded backdrop, meant that all the gods were clamoring

for an audience with her. But Asteria's only thought was for the Titan Perses and with him she had one daughter, the goddess Hecate. Just like her mother, she, too, was interested in the art of prophecy, and together they would delve into the world of divination and predict the fates of humankind.

Despite her alliance with Perses, there were some deities who would not give up trying to snare Asteria for themselves. Zeus, the king of the gods, was one of those. Unable to take his eyes off her, he became besotted with her heavenly allure. So enamored was he that he pursued her through the sky, and this was no delicate affair. He thrashed out his thunderbolts and tore through the clouds, chasing her with such passion that he caused chaos. Luckily Asteria was too quick for him. She did not want to belong to any of the gods, for she knew that ultimately they would steal her brightness and extinguish all the stars. Instead she chose to take control of her own fate. She transformed from a goddess to a quail.

The celestial realm was no place for such a tiny bird, and so, drawn by gravity, she plunged down from the sky, plummeting toward the ocean at such a speed that she would surely have drowned. Even worse, the arms of Poseidon were open and waiting, for he, too, was smitten by her charms.

"What is there to do?" gasped Asteria. "I cannot live in my beloved heavens with the stars, and I cannot fall into the ocean and die a watery death, and if I concede I am trapped forever." And so it was that she transformed once more, and this time she became an island known as Ortygia, "the quail island."

"Here I will stay, floating in the Aegean, and no man will ever make me their own." The island, which was renamed Delos, was dedicated to the goddess by the ancient Greeks. Just as she had looked to the stars and astrology to divine the fortunes of those who sought her blessing, Delos, too, became sacred; a place where the oracle of dreams could be found, and destinies were created. Its beauty was celebrated, and offerings laid in the temples for Asteria, the starry one. For while she no longer lived in the sky, she would always remain a shining star in the hearts and minds of her people.

Asteria

"I light my own path and find a way through the darkness."

GODDESS RITUAL

Shining brightly like the stars, Asteria navigates her way through the night sky. She moves like a shooting star, with grace and speed, and is in charge of her own destiny. Whether she's being chased by the gods or determining the fates of humans, Asteria finds her own way, and trusts that the light within will bring her home.

This ritual, which uses the sky at night, will help to calm your mind so that you'll be able to look on the bright side and feel imbued with positive energy.

* Choose a night when the sky is clear, and you can see the stars from your window.

* Take a long, slow breath in and count to four, then release the breath and count to four again.

* Repeat this breathing cycle and extend your breath by one more beat. Continue to breathe in this way for a minute, until you feel calm.

* Let your gaze soften and look at the sky. Notice the stars twinkling above you. Fix your eyes on one star—it could be the biggest and brightest, or simply one that catches your eye.

* Imagine a stream of light coming down from the star. It reaches down through the heavens and connects to the top of your head.

* This tendril of light is a conduit for the star to send you light and energy.

* See the light pulsating along the thread as it travels through the heavens.

* Feel it hit the top of your head and fill you up with vibrant light.

* Close your eyes, and let the star imbue you with brightness.

* Picture your entire body glowing from head to toe.

Fortuna

Roman Goddess of Fate and Fortune

THEMES
Abundance, fate, gratitude, grace

"THE FARMER'S FATE"

There once lived a farmer, a miserly and bitter man, who did little to help others. While his farm was prosperous and he made good money from his crops, he stashed it away for himself, and while he had an abundance of food that he'd grown, including the milk from his cows, he never gave any of the surplus to the poor and needy. As far as he was concerned the gods had blessed him, and him alone. In return for this good fortune, he would pray to them every night, and in particular he would pray to the goddess Fortuna to secure his luck and ensure that the blessings continued.

In truth, he knew little of the ways of the gods and cared even less about them. As long as he was receiving their favor, then he would sing their praises, but there was no real thought or care behind his words, and he wasn't truly thankful.

For their part, most of the gods barely noticed him. As a man he was not worth acknowledging, but the goddess Fortuna had heard his prayers and watched in amusement every night.

"Can you hear him? He sings to me so sweetly," she would laugh, "but his words are false, and I wonder how he would sing if his fortunes reversed?" Being the goddess of fate and fortune, you might think she had a say in matters, but her powers were unpredictable, and they could go either way with little influence from her. As a way of demonstrating this she would often appear to people, balancing upon a ball. Depending on the way it turned she would either stand or fall to illustrate the fickleness of fate. Not that anyone ever understood. They petitioned her for help but failed to see that she had little to do with their fortunes.

The farmer was the same. He blindly continued in his nightly demonstrations, believing that he was a favorite of hers. So, on the day when everything changed, it came as quite a shock.

It started when his best horse escaped, and then his crops began to wither and die. The milk that he'd taken to market that morning turned sour and he made nothing for his efforts. The humble offerings he did salvage didn't raise a coin.

"Fair goddess, why have you forsaken me? I am your favorite!" he cried that night. "What must I do to win back your love?" It was then that Fortuna appeared to him in a vision. She was standing upon a giant ball. Now, most people might have at least questioned why, but the farmer, who was desperate to turn his luck around, believed it was a sign.

"Ah!" cried the farmer. "I see what you are trying to tell me! This is how you want me to show my love to you!"

The next day he commandeered a giant ball, positioned it in the town square and promptly stood on it. There he balanced for most of the morning, wobbling and teetering in the breeze. As you can imagine, this was something of a spectacle and the townsfolk gathered in their droves. They laughed and they jeered to see this man, who had always been so miserly

and cruel, look so ridiculous. When one of them gave the ball a swift kick, sending it rolling toward the gates at high speed, they laughed even more. When the farmer fell off, their hoots were heard for miles around. Bruised and battered he made his way home, feeling sorry for himself.

"Fortuna, I did what you asked, I showed my love for all to see and this is how you repay me!" Once more the goddess appeared, and this time she was carrying a giant cornucopia filled with fruit, vegetables, and gold coins, an offering of abundance to her people. Like before, she did not say a word, but she didn't have to. Again the farmer's ego was such that he made his own mind up.

"Ah, now I see what you want me to do, to win back your favor."

This would not be easy for him, but if it would turn his fortunes around, then it was worth it.

The next day, he walked back into town, taking with him all his worldly goods, all the food in his larder, and the coins in his pockets. He left them in the square, and the people took their share. They stuffed their pockets and filled their arms. They were incredulous. How could this man who had been so stingy all his life suddenly do this? But still they took it all, believing that at last the goddess Fortuna had blessed them.

That night, with nothing but the clothes upon his back and no family or friends to show for all his years of toil and tantrums, the farmer realized something. Fortune was not something to be bestowed by the deities. It came and it went, and you could not influence it. You could only be thankful when it was your turn, and accepting of your fate when it wasn't.

GODDESS AFFIRMATION
"I embrace the unexpected."

GODDESS RITUAL

Fortuna is the goddess of abundance, and while she has a certain amount of power, she does not control the direction of fate. She is very much concerned with the wheel of life, and how things continue to turn. Fortuna teaches us to embrace the unexpected and go with the flow.

This ritual uses one of her key symbols to help you generate positive energy, attract prosperity, and face the future with optimism. Fortuna's cornucopia is a large horn-shaped container filled with goodies. You're going to create your own cornucopia and fill it with items dear to you. This will remind you that your life is filled with good fortune, which in turn creates more positive energy.

 Find a box that you like and fill it with things that you love. If you prefer, you can use a bowl or a large dish.

* Choose things like crystals, stones, shells, and coins, also mementos like ticket stubs or photographs, from special days.

* Add in your favorite quotes and poems and if you have any special wishes for the future, write them down and add those in.

* You might also want to write down snippets of special memories that you can read through.

* Keep the box somewhere safe and add new things to it regularly, to keep the positive energy flowing.

* Also, make a point of dipping into it at least once a week, to remind yourself of the wonderful twists and turns of fate, and the adventures you've had so far.

Fire and Sun

The deities in this section have one thing in common. They all have a fire in their belly, and a distinctive way of unleashing their shine, from goddesses who carry and protect the sun's light, to fire ladies, and those who govern the hearth and home. Then there are the volcanic lovelies with a volatile temperament and a passionate outlook to match—best not to cross their path on the wrong day for fear of an eruption. That said, they're equally feisty when it comes to protecting their charges, and the earth around them.

Sass is the main order the day with these deities. They may be warriors or witches, but the one thing that makes them stand out is attitude—or cattitude, in the case of some.

They can show you how to step into your power, and radiate light and love, from acknowledging your inner beauty, to being flexible in the face of adversity and harnessing your strength. These vibrant goddesses are the perfect companions for fireside days and sunshine rays—they always know how to ignite the spark within.

Sunna

Norse Goddess of the Sun

THEMES
Joy, determination, positive energy, self-esteem

"DAUGHTER OF FLAME AND ASH"

When you look up and see the sun radiant in all her glory, remember that she does this for you. That every day, she faces the same battle; a tumultuous chase that could lead to her death—but the sacrifice she makes is worth it. The sun sheds her light in golden rays so that you can feel her warmth and she urges you to do the same. For when we unleash our shine, that is when we truly sparkle.

And while she hasn't yet been caught by the slavering wolf at her heels, she has come close, and it could happen almost any time. But to truly understand her plight, you must hear her story.

She was born from the sparks of the Land of Fire, called Muspellsheim at the dawn of time, when there was nothing but a blackened void where the sky might be, during the fall of the great giant Ymir. His lifeless form could have hung in the ether for an eternity, but the Norse gods had other ideas. Odin, the great father of all, and his cohorts Vili and Ve, decided to create the world from his broken body. But for the world to truly come to life it needed light in all its forms, and so Odin picked a spark and rolled it between his fingers. He held it close to his mouth and whispered sacred words, breathed life into the fiery ball, and the goddess Sunna was born.

A golden-haired beauty and daughter of flame and ash, she was a majestic sight, and both gods and humans alike were in awe of her power. While the goddess loved such adoration, she was practical, too. She knew that her role was to ride through the sky on her chariot every day and keep the fiery orb burning. She also knew that her vibrant light would attract predators, and that evil lurked in the shadows in the form of the dark wolf Skoll. She could feel

his hot breath upon her neck, the snap of his jaws rang in her ears, and sometimes she even imagined the sharp bristle of his fur against her skin. He wanted to steal her light, to swallow it whole and bring about the end of the world, but she would not let that happen. She urged Odin to help her, to give her speed to flee the beast.

"I need horses that are fleet of foot, which can rise before the dawn and cross the sky in the blink of an eye. Steeds that will not let me down." And so it was that Sunna received two such magical creatures, known as Allsvinn, meaning "very fast," and Arvak, whose name meant "early rising." Their mission was to carry the goddess and her chariot through the sky safely, and even when the wolf nipped at their heels, to keep going, to fly faster, and reach the other side before dusk.

Some might have waned in their purpose, for it was a daily battle. The chase would never end, and Skoll would never give up until he'd claimed his prize. His eyes burned red with lust for the sun goddess, but he never quite reached her, until one fateful day.

As always, the chase began in earnest. Sunna bursting into action, rising up toward the heavens with Skoll in hot pursuit. Her rays blazed through the sky, burning a path that, from earth, looked like the most glorious sunrise. But it was a long and arduous journey, and as the hours bled on, the wolf gathered speed. Today he felt different, today he had a chance. He lashed out with his clawed feet, he let the wind carry him forward until Sunna was almost within his grasp. He let out an almighty howl, which split the heavens in two, and opened his mouth wide.

Sunna could feel his presence looming above her, and she knew in that moment that there was little she could do. Horror coiled within her stomach; her light was about to be extinguished and she had failed her people. The wolf clamped down with his jaws, and Sunna was gone. Daylight became night and the earth was plunged into darkness. But this was not the end. Her loyal horses would not let Skoll win. They dug deep and with all their supernatural strength they pulled, dragging Sunna from his clutches once more. The wolf tried to hold on, but his chance was gone and she slipped away.

The sky lit up once more. The world was saved, and upon the earth those who watched claimed they had seen the most extraordinary of visions; an eclipse. But you and I know the truth. We know it was the daughter of flame and ash upon her trusty steeds, doing what she must to shine her light for us.

"I shine my light and unleash my inner radiance."

GODDESS RITUAL

Beautiful Sunna knows there is power and strength in being who you are meant to be. Learning to love yourself is the key, and this self-assured goddess uses this strength to shine and bathe the world in light.

This ritual, which uses the vibrant light of the sun, will help to turn up your shine, and boost self-esteem.

✳ Stand beneath the light of the sun. If it's not possible to do this outside, position yourself near a window.

✳ Imagine a cord of light extending out from your solar plexus, which is the area just above your naval. This cord is attached to the heart of the sun.

✳ Every time you breathe in you draw golden energy along the cord, and into your solar plexus.

✳ As you exhale, this energy floods the rest of your body, filling you with vitality and confidence.

✳ Continue to breathe deeply, drawing the sun's energy toward you. At the same time picture the sun getting bigger and brighter, as if it's also being pulled into your orbit.

✳ To finish, imagine that the sun's light encases you from head to toe.

Pele

Goddess of Fire, Volcanoes, and Dance

THEMES
Passion, protection, freedom, honor

"THE DANCE OF LIFE"

From the first day that she emerged from her mother's womb, Pele's plaintive cry could be heard. As beautiful as it was shrill, it marked her entrance into the world of men, a place where she would find her feet and shape her own kingdom. Born to the fertility goddess Haumea on the island of Tahiti, Pele was different to the rest of the family for she had a warrior's heart and a fire within that glowed brightly. She was wild and free and did not care for rules or limitations. Each day was an adventure, an opportunity to carve her own path, which she did without thought or remorse. It wasn't that she didn't prize love above all other things; if anything, she loved too much. Her passions were the driving force behind everything she did. When something caught her eye, it could not be unseen. If it piqued her interest, it was hers for she would seek it out obsessively, making it her sole mission. And while her interests were many, it was true love that called to her the most.

But while Pele was led by her passions, her sister Namakaokahai was fueled by all that was calm and balanced. She was the goddess of the sea, and she took her responsibility seriously, keeping the waters smooth and abundant with marine life. Her serene beauty was renowned across the land, and while Pele's fiery spirit was admonished, Namakaokahai was honored. No doubt this caused a feud, which started as a gentle and playful trickle between siblings and grew into a river, then a sea. When Namakaokahai finally took a husband in the charming sorcerer Aukelenuiaiku, Pele was jealous. She wanted the attention for herself. After all, wasn't she the most magnificent deity in the known universe? Didn't she deserve adoration, too?

It wasn't that she wanted to cause waves or fan the flames of desire. Pele had little understanding of what was to come or how her actions might impact others. To her, life was a game and she would dance through each chapter with wild abandon. It was this lithe and sensuous movement that stole the heart of her sister's husband. A torrid affair ensued, and Aukelenuiaiku was smitten. Swallowed by the heat of Pele's advances, he lost himself in her arms. But while the lovers were oblivious, the first rumblings of descent could be felt.

Pele's father, the great creator god Kane Miloha'i, could see everything, and he was angry. He hurled a torrent of abuse upon his daughter, sending her into exile for her thoughtless deeds. But that wasn't enough for Namakaokahai. Vitriol swelled within her, and the once tranquil waters broke apart as she unleashed her wrath. Everywhere Pele fled she followed, sending a deluge of watery destruction that swallowed every last bit of earth. In response, Pele unleashed her fire. She fed the flames within, opening great chasms that she filled with her lava. She moved from place to place, never resting, for she would not let them banish her completely. Yes, she had succumbed to her cravings, but what is life if it is not to be seized and enjoyed? Pele wouldn't go quietly.

She fought back, and forged ahead, making a place for herself in the world where no one could dictate her future. She came to an island, carved out great bubbling craters and filled them with the scorching liquid of her desire. She wandered the island, living and breathing in every particle of dust, every rock and crumbling stone, making it her own. Her Hawai'i, her home.

Pele chose the high mountains of Mauna Loa to finally settle. From this vantage point, she could keep a watchful eye upon her sister, knowing that her waves could not possibly reach her. Pele was safe, and free, but she was not done. This was her island and refuge, and it meant more to her than anything else. She had swapped one passion for another, and in her homeland she found strength and honor. She treasured each grain of sand; protected each lump of rock and rugged clump of earth. Should one of her people dare to steal from this place, they would feel her burning touch upon their skin, but if they acted with respect and love, they were rewarded. If they followed their heart's desires, and trod lightly upon the land, danced to the tune of their dreams and the sweet rhythm of her heart, Madame Pele, as she was known, would take them by the hand and join them in a warm embrace.

"I follow my passion, and act with honor and integrity."

GODDESS RITUAL

Fiery and feisty, Pele is a proud goddess. She feels deeply, loves deeply, and protects what she holds dear. She is not afraid to stand her ground, and she always acts from a place of truth and honor. She can help you draw strength and assert yourself when faced with a difficult situation.

This ritual works with the element of fire to fuel you with passion and courage.

✳ Start by thinking about a situation that fills you with fear. Do not dwell on the feeling, simply bring it to the forefront of your mind.

✳ Say, "I've got this!" loudly and with passion, even if you don't feel like it.

✳ Take a deep breath and begin by rubbing the palms of your hands together to create friction. Do this for at least a minute.

✳ When you're ready, draw your hands apart slowly and you should feel a slight pull from the energy that you have created.

✳ Imagine that this is a ball of fire, and you are holding it between both hands. Draw the ball toward you, until it expands and completely encircles you in a fiery bubble.

✳ Breathe deeply, and let the flames engulf you.

✳ Picture hot lava traveling through your veins, filling you with passion and strength.

✳ Spend a couple of minutes reveling in these feelings. Know that you are powerful and protected. Any negative energy directed at you will be repelled by the flames.

✳ Whenever you feel vulnerable, rub your hands together and create the ball of fire, then let the energy fill you up.

Vesta

Roman Goddess of Hearth and Home

THEMES
Generosity, focus, family, abundance

"AND ALL BECAUSE SHE CARED..."

Before the much-loved pantheon of deities in ancient Rome, there came the mighty Titans, a group charged with power, and hungry for more. While they lived and loved like other gods, their leader Kronos was besieged by jealousy and petrified he might lose his throne, so much so that when his gorgeous wife Rhea gave birth to a child, he would swallow it whole. His mind was a whirling vortex of anxiety, and when the voices came, they whispered of betrayal among his children. The only way to assure that his reign continued and quell the madness was to take the very thing he loved and steal away its breath.

Vesta was his firstborn, a beautiful girl with a kind and generous spirit, and so she was swallowed first, but her destiny was not to languish in the pit of his stomach. Thanks to the wily deeds of her brother Jupiter, she and all her siblings were eventually freed, and being first swallowed, she was the last one to escape. As such she was considered both the oldest and youngest of the gods.

Stunning in face and form, Vesta turned many heads, and her admirers were numerous, including the gods Apollo and Neptune, but Vesta wasn't interested. Her heart was by the hearth, and her mind was with family, for to her that was the most important thing in the kingdom. She longed to provide a safe haven, a place of security and abundance where bonds could be formed, where everyone could gather together.

The deities had other ideas. Their titanic squabbles rocked the heavens. Whether governed by desire, jealousy, or just the need for power, their frustrations bubbled deep, and the thunder clouds gathered.

"Why?" Vesta would ask her brother Jupiter. "What is the purpose of this? I do not understand."

"You are sweet in spirit and quite unlike the others," he would reply. "They do not care about each other—they want what they want, and they each want to be the most powerful."

Vesta would sigh, "Then I must do what I can to help. I will not take a husband; I refuse to choose and add to the turmoil. Instead, I will stay by your side, and look after your home. I will honor your hearth with fire, and I will bake your bread. I will create a space where they can be together, where all conflict can be set aside. I will keep the home fires burning."

And this she did with passion. She cleaned and cared for the home and did all she could to make the place welcoming, but still the deities would not come. They were so opposed to each other and consumed with their own greed, they failed to realize what they really needed was to unite and focus on building a family. This troubled Vesta greatly, but she would not give up trying.

"I will create a hearth, and fill it with fire. It will be the warmest, most abundant place, and everyone who sees it and feels the heat will draw near."

And with a click of her fingers, she ignited the spark that would grow into a flame. She nurtured the fire within with all her might. She watched the embers glow, and cajoled them with her powers, until what started as a simple hearth fire became a vibrant beacon and a symbol of strength and harmony.

And slowly, one by one, the gods cast aside their differences and came to the door. They wiped their feet and bowed their heads, as a mark of respect. They entered cautiously, drawn like moths by the golden flames. They didn't understand what was so mesmerizing, but they felt it inside, and as that warmth grew, so, too, did their need to reach out, to break bread together and drink wine. Soon they were talking, sharing tales of victory and words of encouragement. They were laughing heartily at each other's jokes, and offering support, a hand, an arm around the shoulder, or simply a smile that said everything. Once more they were a family, a tight unit that was happy to be together.

Vesta smiled. "Wherever there is a hearth for family and friends to gather, there is a home."

This was a fact that all the people of ancient Rome agreed upon. Nothing was more important than a glowing hearth and the warm embrace of family. And so it was that the beautiful, virginal Vesta was to be one of the most powerful and important deities of the time, and all because she cared.

"I let the generosity of my spirit warm those I meet."

GODDESS RITUAL

Vesta had a heart of gold, and the power of fire at her fingertips. Her people petitioned her daily to keep the hearth burning and their family safe. Being associated with baking, she was also linked to abundance and prosperity. If you were in need, Vesta was the loving deity who could help change your fortunes.

This ritual, which works with the element of fire, will help you to feel safe and loved, and manifest abundance.

You'll need a fireproof bowl, some matches, paper, and a pen.

* To start, think about the things that make you feel vulnerable—perhaps certain situations make you feel more exposed, like when you're meeting new people, or it could be that attention makes you feel uncomfortable.

* Write a couple of words on a small piece of paper to summarize your thoughts.

* Fold the paper, take a match, and set it alight.

* Drop the burning paper into the fireproof bowl and watch as your insecurities turn to smoke.

* Next, think about what you'd like to attract more of—for example, you might want more opportunities for growth, or to boost your finances.

* Think of a couple of words to represent this and write them on another piece of paper.

* Fold and burn the paper in the fireproof bowl. As you do, gaze into the smoke and say, "Take the bad away, by ash and flame, bring forth the good, by Vesta's name."

* To finish, let all the contents of the bowl burn to ash, then scatter this away and repeat the affirmation.

Inanna

Sumerian Goddess of Love, Fertility, and Sensuality

THEMES
Balance, tenacity, unity, love

"THE QUEEN OF HEAVEN AND EARTH"

Beneath that which we know, there is that which we don't, also known as the Great Below, or the Underworld, in ancient Sumer. It was a shadowy realm where the souls of the dead were sent to appease the gods, and yet there were glimmers of light, too—tales that reveal a different side to the unseen. While most of the deities preferred to keep their feet above ground, there was one who dared to walk beyond the line and venture into unknown territory; a powerful goddess, who had no fear of the mysteries of the deep. Her name was Inanna, although some knew her as Ishtar.

Queen of Heaven and Earth, she reigned supreme and governed all matters of the heart, for love was important to this deity and she embraced her feminine wiles with relish, having taken many lovers. As such, she became the goddess of love and sensuality, the one who brides would call upon on their wedding night, and the being who could grant fertility. And, just as love has a less pleasurable flip side, so, too, did this queen, for she also governed war. Whether it was war between the sheets or great nations, she had her hand in the conflict and loved nothing more than to stir the pot.

To be fair, there is only so much fun you can have while straddling heaven and earth, and Inanna wanted more! And so it was that she decided to venture from the sky to the Great Below to visit her sister the Queen of the Dead, who had recently lost her husband. While most would be fooled by what seemed like an innocent trip to console her bereaved sibling, Inanna's nearest and dearest knew her better. On hearing that she had arrived at the entrance to the Underworld, her sister Ereshkigal locked all the seven gates that visitors had to pass through. She gave strict

instructions that Inanna could only enter if she sacrificed something of herself.

Never one to be unprepared or deterred, Inanna had come adorned in regal finery, including her crown of heaven, golden ring, beads, scepter, breastplate, and rod of power. It was to be expected that such a mighty deity would be dripping in jewels, even if it was inappropriate for the journey.

She knocked loudly at each door.

"Let me in, let me in. I am Inanna, Queen of Heaven and Earth!" she cried.

Her wrath at being shut out grew keen and sharp, but her determination to enter surpassed any fury, so at each she offered a gift—a ring or some beads, her scepter, breastplate, rod, and finally her crown of heaven. When it came to the last gate, the one that would grant her access to this new kingdom, she gave the only thing she had left—the robes that clung to her body.

This amused Ereshkigal much, who was not surprised at her sister's tenacity. Even so, she would not let her get the upper hand, and as there was no love lost between the two, she set her with a death stare that silenced Inanna's beating heart, turning her into a corpse.

An abrupt end for a heavenly queen, but not the end of the tale for Inanna. Ever resourceful and always organized, she had given her servants strict instructions on what to do if she didn't return. After seeking help from her father, the god Enki, Inanna's body was eventually retrieved from the Underworld, and revived with the food and water of life. She rose from the dead like a phoenix from its ashes. Some said she was even more beautiful than before, and some said, even more deadly.

But as with all things, there is a balance to life and death, a truth which Inanna had always known. When a soul comes back to life, something must be done to redress the balance, otherwise the veil between heaven and earth is disturbed, and chaos ensues. For her part she knew she had to send someone to the other side in her place, but who?

Fate was to provide the perfect solution. When Inanna arrived back at her palace, she found her children and friends were still in mourning, adorned in sack cloth as a mark of respect for their loss, but her lover Dumuzi was dressed in his best, and celebrating upon the throne. As revenge, he was thrown into the Great Below to repent for his behavior.

Some might assume this was the plan all along, but we will never really know, for it is foolish to question the gods, and reckless to challenge a woman in love—especially if that woman is the Queen of Heaven and Earth.

"Every moment is an opportunity to restore balance."

GODDESS RITUAL

Inanna's descent into the Underworld is fraught with conflict, and while it doesn't end well, her tenacious spirit means that in the end she is reborn and able to find some peace. In this story, she illustrates the power of resilience, and of searching for balance, even in the most troubling of times.

This ritual takes inspiration from Inanna's offerings at the seven gates to help you feel grounded, and find some balance whenever you need it.

You'll need a treasured item. This could be a piece of jewelry that means something, a token, or a memento from a time when you felt content and at peace.

✳ Find a comfortable space where you won't be disturbed.

✳ Light a white candle as a symbol of the light in the dark of the Underworld.

✳ Take some deep breaths to calm your mind, then hold your treasured item in both hands. Close your eyes and breathe in the emotions associated with it. Relive them in your mind and enjoy those feelings of peace.

✳ Place the object in front of the candle and say, "Like a light in the dark, as this candle shines, let this be an amulet to soothe my mind. A gift to help me find my way and bring balance into every day."

✳ Let the candle burn down, then retrieve your object and hold it whenever you need to recreate a sense of peace.

Brigid

Celtic Goddess of Fire and Healing

THEMES
Healing, inspiration, rebirth, wisdom

"THE BRIGHT ONE"

When the sun rises on the first day of spring and the belly of the earth is pregnant with new life, that is when you feel her near. Her gentle healing touch comes in a tender tendril of breeze, and when she wraps her arms around you, you feel exhilarated and ready for anything. For she is Brigid, goddess of healing and inspiration, and her creative energy is rife, at the beginning of the wheel of the year.

Daughter of the Tuatha Dé Dannan, a magical race who lived in the mystical lands of the West, Brigid was born of their leaders Dagda and Danu. She emerged at the point when the sun was about to rise, which explains the fiery rays of her hair, which stretch forever onward. And just like the tempestuous heat of the sun, Brigid grew to be a woman of contradiction. When she loved, she loved with passion, but anger the goddess and you will see sparks fly. There is fire at the heart of this beauty, and she was drawn to the hearth, and smithcraft.

While the flames burned bright, making her Brigid "the Bright One," exalted among her people, she was also drawn to water. Rivers, streams, and sacred wells were her home, and people would flock to these sites in the hope that they might meet her.

To see her in her maiden form was to be given a gift and, depending on her mood, you might leave feeling refreshed, inspired, or simply with an insight that could turn your life around. But as generous as she could be, Brigid never suffered fools, and those who might chance their arm thinking they were better than others would do well to heed this tale.

For there were once two beggars, one a kind man suffering with leprosy, the other, a thief with a crafty heart

and mind. Both had come to the stream of Saint Brigid's Holy Well in Ireland, believing it to be blessed with magical powers. The first neither expected to be healed or receive a gift—he was simply hoping for a moment of peace and respite among the pain. The second was hoping for divine intervention, and to make his fortune from the tale he would tell. Although they did not come together, they were both there at the sacred moment when Brigid chose to emerge.

Charging toward the goddess came the second man, the stronger of the two, knocking the other out of the way. Cup in hand, he was ready to ask for his desires while the first bowed his head low, his deformed face skimming the water.

Brigid smiled, and dipped her finger into the inky depths, causing gentle ripples that spread outward like the rays of her light. The water glistened with healing energy that soothed the skin of the leper, and soon began to transform his appearance. He looked in amazement at his flesh, examining each limb with tears of joy.

"You have healed me; how can I ever thank you?"

Brigid spoke then, and her words filled his heart with happiness and his head with such beautiful poetry. "Now your outward appearance reflects your spirit within.

Live a good and earnest life and be happy. That is thanks enough." The man nodded. So filled with emotion was he that he clung to the earth and wept with joy.

The second, wily beggar jostled for her attention, rising up in her face and waving his hands.

"Sweet Brigid, oh how wonderful and radiant you are! How I adore you, oh bright one. Please, I beg you, bless me also with your magic for I deserve it too."

"I will," she smiled, urging him to dip his fingers into the waters, but instead of some miracle overcoming him, his skin began to transform, his limbs began to twist and his face grimaced in horror.

"What befalls me?" he gasped. His words caught in his throat. "What have you done?"

"Only what you asked," said Brigid sweetly. "You asked for my magic, but you did so with little respect and darkness in your heart, so the magic you received was tinged with it. Now your outward appearance also reflects your spirit within."

"But you've turned me into a leper!" he screamed. "How could you do this?"

Brigid paused, glanced at the man before her and left him with this one thought; "If you can bring yourself to change your heart, then your appearance will follow suit."

With that she turned and disappeared. Just as spring fades into summer, and the wheel of the year turns, so the goddess known as "the Bright One," and the fire of the hearth and inspiration, returned to the earth, ready to be reborn.

"The spark of inspiration burns within me."

GODDESS RITUAL

A complex deity, Brigid was many things to many people. Her themes are wide and varied, but there is creativity at the heart of everything she does, from her ability to create new life, to her fires that shaped tools in the hearth, and the inspiration she gave to poets and artists. Brigid's most loved for her healing powers, which can bring about transformation.

This ritual, which combines the elements of fire and water, will help to cleanse and heal body and mind.

You will need an oil burner, a little water, some orange-scented oil, and a tea light. Orange is associated with the power of the sun and the element of fire.

- To start, add some water to your oil burner, light the tea light inside, and add three or four drops of the scented oil.

- Close your eyes and inhale the sweet aroma. Draw it in deep, and, as you exhale, let your body relax. Feel your limbs loosen and let any heaviness float away.

- Imagine that with every breath, the orange-scented oil infuses your aura, the energy field around your body, with vitality. It cleanses your body and mind, driving out negative energy and replacing it with joy.

- To take this a step further, you can repeat the ritual and add some of the infused water to your bath, then inhale the aroma as you soak.

Kali

Hindu Goddess of Time and Death

THEMES
Change, perception, intuition, new beginnings

"DEATH BECOMES HER"

There once lived a goddess who was much misunderstood. A goddess so powerful, she controlled the parameters of time; a primordial being whose true nature was divine but whose appearance was demonic. An earth mother, a warrior, both feral and loving, she embodied every aspect, allowing her followers to see that she was neither good nor bad, but a combination of both. And while all these things made her special and strong, still people feared her, and in this they were wrong.

They looked only at the surface, at what they could see—at her terrifying appearance—and while most would agree she was hardly endearing, this goddess was not who they should have been fearing. For humankind is often blinded by what they perceive to be acceptable, and should someone be fair of face, they're likely to be seen as kind and good. Whereas poor Kali, for that was her name, was considered demonic in her appearance and misunderstood.

Savage, and terrifying, it's true that to cross her path you might incur her wrath, but only if your heart is dark. In truth, Kali delivered her punishment as a way of bringing about change, cutting away the dead to reveal the living, breathing, truth at everything's heart. For in change there is a death of sorts, an ending that paves the way for a new beginning, and Kali recognized that endings could be born out of pain. She, unlike many other deities, knew that life was far from easy for her people, and her main mission was to protect them; to slice away the debris and free them from the things holding them back.

And so it was that Kali was the one called upon at the great battle of Durga. Such was her wrath against all evil

beings that she sprang forth from the head of the warrior goddess Durga to fight and defeat the Buffalo Demon. She was the one who brought salvation. With her blue-black skin, and her three wild eyes, she struck terror into the hearts of the demons. With her girdle of severed arms and her garland of fifty skulls, not to mention her tongue, ever long and slavering, she was the one to spill their blood. When the dying was done and the monsters slayed, she was the one who danced upon their bodies. With her arms in the air and her hair flowing free, she was feral, and jubilant. And why shouldn't she be? After all it was her who had saved the day.

While she danced, and danced upon the cremation ground, there were those who looked on in horror. Such was her frenzy that the bones of the dead, which were ground to dust, were not the only victims beneath her frenetic form. And in that moment, Kali saw her husband Shiva "The Destroyer of Darkness" and god of all creation lying prostrate beneath her feet. Pale of skin, and a picture of stillness, he was the carpet upon which she stood. Once more, you might wonder where is the good.

But the truth is, death becomes her; just as life, and its formation, becomes Shiva. She is dark, he is light, but together they fight to protect their people. The two reflect different sides of each other, and the point therein is that Shiva cannot be seen without Kali at his side. She is the living force of his power and energy, and not simply his bride.

To this day, she is revered and feared in equal amounts, but for those who can look beyond the surface and see the truth within, they will know that she is working to free them of sin and give them a new beginning. So I offer you a challenge as you read this tale. Take a deep breath and look into her eye of wisdom, cast aside the veil of doubt that colors your perception. Be truthful with yourself and others, and do not let misdirection lead you down a false path.

For if you do, you may find yourself facing your own demons, backed into a corner with nowhere to run. You may realize that what truly matters is not the way things appear, but the way things are, not sweet words that are easily said, but those actions done from the heart. And when the monsters surround you, their mouths gaping and ready to swallow you whole, in that moment of darkness as the shadows crawl upon your skin, that is when you'll pray for the goddess Kali to save you from sin.

Kali

"I embrace the light and dark in my life, for together they make me whole."

GODDESS RITUAL

Kali's appearance is terrifying, but beneath the surface, she is a loving, protecting deity. She governs time and change, and shows us that to move forward, we often need to release the past and experience a death of sorts so that we can start afresh. Kali's eye of wisdom allows her access to the truth, and she urges us to also trust our intuition and see beyond the superficial.

This ritual, which focuses on the third eye chakra, helps to trigger your intuition, so that you'll be able to look at things from a different perspective and also gain a deeper understanding of yourself and others.

The third eye chakra is located in the middle of the forehead, and it is the seat of your intuition.

- Find a quiet place to sit, where you won't be disturbed. Light a white candle to represent the positive aspects of your personality, and a black candle to represent your shadow self, the darker side of your psyche.

- Consider how the two work together to form a whole, just as the darker and lighter aspects of your makeup create balance.

- Close your eyes and, with your index finger, begin to gently trace a circular pattern in the center of your forehead. Imagine you are outlining an eye shape and continue to massage this area for at least a minute.

- When you're ready, open your eyes and gaze into both flames.

- Let any thoughts or insights come to you. Don't force things; let your natural intuition do the work and if nothing comes, that's fine.

- This is a ritual that you can practice every day, and eventually you will notice that your sixth sense begins to flow, and you will gain a deeper understanding of yourself and others.

Saule

Baltic Sun Goddess

THEMES
Gratefulness, selflessness,
joy, kindness

**"WHY THE MOON
HAS WRINKLES"**

Once upon a time there was a sun goddess, a hardworking, generous being, with a crown of light around her head. When she smiled it was like the rising sun, and when she laughed, her rays spread far and wide in every direction. Never one to complain, she knew the role she played was important to her people, and so each day at dawn she would awaken, peering into the horizon. She'd stretch, and her fingers would paint the sky in orange and yellow patterns. Then she would go to her chariot and polish its copper wheels. There was nothing she loved more than to ride it through the sky and watch the people below stare in wonder. And it wasn't because she wanted their adoration, it was simply the fact that she could provide some light and warmth in their life.

"Another day!" she would whisper to her beautiful horses, and they would whinny with pleasure, for they, too, felt the same way. Strong and steadfast, her stallions were magical creatures, and her closest companions. They pulled her chariot with all their might, and even on the longest of days they did not waver. Their focus was on the job in hand and pleasing their mistress. It might seem extraordinary that they never tired, nor did they sweat, but when you enjoy every moment of a task it no longer feels like work.

Each day was the same, and while some of the more demanding deities might have something to say about this, Saule was truly thankful for she had realized a long time ago that happiness is a choice and that small delights make all the difference.

Her husband, the moon god Mēness, was less enamored with his wife's responsibilities. Governed by his moods and emotions, he was constantly changing, shifting from

one shape to another out of boredom. He cared less about the people, and casting light into their world, so his glow was translucent and not always present to the naked eye. But for Saule, there was much goodness to be found on earth. After all, it was their union that birthed the stars and planets in the first place.

"I will never understand why you do this every day," he would sneer. "You do not have to. You are a goddess, you can do what you want."

Saule would smile sweetly. "But this is what I want to do."

Mēness would frown and shake his head. "I do not understand you."

"You are the moon, and I am the sun," she would say in reply.

"We are not meant to understand each other, we are meant to exist and that is all." The conversation would end there, but the subject was not forgotten and caused much consternation on the part of Mēness.

Every day, after riding tirelessly through the fiery landscape of the heavens, Saule would settle upon a hill, near the edge of the ocean and there she would rest and wash her horses in the sea. Holding their golden reins loosely, she would allow them to wander and flex their legs, while she surveyed her kingdom. And it was in these moments during dusk that she would find

peace, and the golden crown that she wore on her head would slowly transform. It would darken in color to form a red ball of light, which consumed her in its glow.

Finally, after taking her time to enjoy the last moments of the day, she would arrive at her silver castle in the sky where she settled with her trusty steeds, ready to make the journey again in the morning.

It was on one such evening that the moon, in his exasperation, challenged his wife once more. "If you were to give up just one day, and spend it with me, do you think it would matter? Could you not sacrifice that to be with your husband? Am I not important to you too?"

Saule shook her head, and flecks of golden light peppered the sky. "Perhaps, when the sun meets the moon during an eclipse, we can share a tender moment, but you must understand that you are my husband, and they," she said pointing to the earth, "are my children. They will always come first. There is no choice or sacrifice to be made. This is the life we have chosen. Instead of grumbling, wouldn't it be much nicer to be grateful for what you have?"

The moon grimaced—the expression he pulled must surely have cracked his face and goes some way to explain why the moon has so many lines and craters upon its surface. Of course, we'll never know the truth of it. That is a secret shared between them, but for her part Saule laughed, and the sound she made reverberated in a wheel of light that spun effortlessly through the cosmos.

"Each moment offers an opportunity to be grateful."

GODDESS RITUAL

Saule is the epitome of contentment. She finds joy in the little things and is grateful for every second of her existence. While she has a job to do, it is not a chore. This is because she recognizes there is power in giving, and that kindness to others, and yourself, is the ultimate gift.

This ritual, which promotes the power of gratitude, should be carried out every day for at least a week. It will boost positive energy, helping to find joy in every moment. You will need a notebook and a pen.

* At the start of the day, as you get out of bed, place your feet firmly on the floor and say, "I embrace the day, and whatever comes my way!" See the day ahead as a clean slate and be thankful for the opportunity to create something new.

* In the evening, when you are relaxing, take a notebook and pen and write down three things that you are grateful for. These can be small things that have happened during the day, like that first cup of coffee on your way to work, or bigger things like spending time with your family.

* Repeat this practice daily, and at the end of the week read back through your notebook.

* Look at the lists of things you are grateful for, and you'll notice a pattern. You'll recognize what gives your life meaning and you'll also see that there are joyful moments in every day.

Bast

Egyptian Sun Goddess and Protector of Cats and Women

THEMES
Power, pleasure, flexibility, self-expression

"THE HEART STEALER"

She moves like lightning, leading the shadows in a merry dance. She is lithe limbed and ready to attack, or flee, depending on the situation. She is a heart stealer; a slayer of demons and she is everywhere. You'll see her in the corner of your eye, so fast that she might only appear to be a blur of breeze; such is her power and ease of movement. She cannot be caught, though many have tried over the years. Her sinewy frame means she can slip through your fingers, like the air. Just as well, for without her many would suffer. She is a fierce protectress, and those under her guard know she will go to the ends of the earth, the tip of heaven, to keep them safe. A champion of women, she will be at your side if you call. She will strengthen your resolve and bolster your courage when all else fails.

You'll find her at the heart of ancient Egypt. She wanders the dusty streets, neither noticed nor appraised, perfectly disguised in her cat-like form; still revered, of course, because that is a part of her legacy. Her followers know that should they harm a hair on the head of her feline friends, they will suffer a punishment worse than death. Cats are gods; it has long been accepted in this part of the world. And she is the greatest of them all.

While you can look for her, you will never find her. She has to find you, to seek you out when you least expect it, when you need comfort or the right words to feel strong. She is there at your side; you'll feel her gentle touch as she brushes against you. In childbirth, when the pain grows too much to bear, she is there, her sweet breath cooling the brow of each new mother, and if you're feeling vulnerable, a woman alone in the night, she will guide you. Her warmth is enough to melt the hardest of hearts. But should

you ignore her, or even worse, treat her ill, then you will pay the price. You'll feel the sting of her claws as they flay your skin, and you'll pray for release.

They call her the perfumed protectress, a heavenly spirit and cohort of the sun god Ra, who is also her father. Together they ride his chariot through the sky, being chased by the serpent Apep as it tries to swallow the sun. But there is no need to fear, for she would never let this monster steal the light. It is her life's work to save the earth and keep evil at bay. This she does every day, for when the sun disappears over the horizon, that is when she gathers her strength and her cat-like wiles and chases the demon away. That is when she follows the slithery path of his scent to a cave far up in the mountains.

Slowly, steadily, and with infinite precision, she leaps from rock to rock, scaling the surface like she is in a dance, for in reality she is playing a part. Then, just as the beast stirs, she will pounce and slaughter him, her sharpened claws ready to prize his skin apart. Each time he dies, as the world is plunged into darkness and we sleep safe in our beds, but by morning the serpent is reborn, and the game begins

once more. But Bast, for that is her name, is more than ready. She likes playing games, particularly those where she gets to hunt her prey. And it is not always straightforward; she, too, will bleed but her blood is true and blue, and as it falls it changes to turquoise, vibrant and filled with light, just like her power.

A woman, a cat, a cat-headed deity, a being of the sun and the Eye of Ra. It doesn't matter how you see her, but you will see her, this I can assure you for she is in every feline that crosses your path; every raggedy urchin that begs at your door. She is in the beautiful breeds, and the flea-bitten fur balls, the ones that shy away, and the ones that lash out in fear. She is there when they purr and there when the fur is flying, and she knows what is in your heart too, whether you mean her harm or care.

She can read it all from your stare. Just look into her hypnotic eyes and let her read your mind. But be prepared. She is a ninja, a warrior, a lover, and a dancer.

And most of all, she is an assassin of the night.

She will steal your heart.

"I approach every day with flexibility and renewed strength."

GODDESS RITUAL

Bast, or Bastet as she was often called, lived life to the full. A pleasure-seeking feisty deity who wasn't afraid to express herself, whether that was in her unique appearance, or the way she moved. Bast teaches us that flexibility is key, and that we shouldn't be afraid to express our individuality.

This ritual, which uses turquoise, the stone most associated with this goddess, will help you find your unique voice and express yourself clearly and creatively.

You will need a piece of turquoise and a light scarf (chiffon or silk, for example). This ritual is best performed when you need to express yourself in some way, perhaps at a meeting, presentation, or in a situation where you need to get your point of view across.

✴ Sit upon the floor and spread the scarf out in front of you.

✴ Cup the turquoise in both hands, close your eyes, and breathe deeply. Ask the stone to infuse you with its creative energy. Turquoise is associated with self-expression and can help you find the right words when you're struggling to speak up.

✴ Let any thoughts flow through your mind—don't try and control them, simply be aware of them.

✴ Notice any feelings that arise while you are holding the stone. You may even hear a conversation forming in your mind or snippets of thoughts, or ideas that you can use when you need to express yourself.

✴ When your mind has quietened, place the turquoise in the center of the scarf, then cover it over, as if you're wrapping it into a small bundle.

✴ Leave the stone here while you record any feelings or insights from earlier, then retrieve the stone and wear the scarf loosely around your neck.

Amaterasu

Shintu Goddess of the Sun

THEMES
Joy, self-esteem, positive energy, rejuvenation

"LADY OF LIGHT"

When dawn breaks upon the rice fields in the Shintu valley, it is a breath of fresh air and a reason for celebration. It is an awakening, as the golden orb of fire that is the sun begins to rise and the first gentle rays of light blend with the horizon. It is a herald of blessings to come, and it is never taken for granted, because the people of that valley remember a time way back when the sun was gone for good.

It wasn't that it was stolen, as so often happens in folk tales, or swallowed by some otherworldly being. It was worse than that. The great lady of light, the goddess Amaterasu, had lost her way. The joy that lived within her heart had been extinguished, and with it, the radiant life-giving force that shone from every pore. She was hollow, breathless, a rock turned to ash by the dark deeds of those around her. As you might imagine, it would take a lot to put out that particular flame. It is something only those nearest and dearest can do, for they have the power to hurt more than most.

Amaterasu's weakness was her brother Susanoo, a boisterous young deity with no respect for the people who worshipped him. A constant source of pain, he did everything in his power to be disruptive, and when that didn't work, he went on an almighty rampage. He destroyed the rice fields that had been carefully tended by the people. He flayed a horse and hurled the dead carcass at Amaterasu's cherished weaving loom, breaking it into pieces, and he slaughtered one of her attendants, out of malice. There was no thought or love, and no repentance. Susanoo didn't care for the lives of others, or the impact of his actions. His heart was a crumbling stone, and his deeds were blackened by the dust of the dead.

But where Susanoo felt nothing, Amaterasu felt everything. The pain was searing, scorching the flesh from her bones, and her heart had been broken in two. When she looked at the valley below, no longer did she see hope. To her it was a place of desolation, and this weighed heavy upon her. She could not see a way forward, an action that would make things right for her people. The despair that Susanoo had placed within consumed her. And so Amaterasu hid away. She found a cave in the highest mountain, a place so remote it would easily swallow her light and, using her heavenly powers, she rolled a stone over the entrance so that no one could get in. Here in the gloom she would reside and repent for her brother's sins.

What she failed to realize was that in her absence the world suffered even more. No longer did the sun rise, casting those first rays upon the earth and bathing the crops in its generous glow. No longer did the heat warm the soil and feed the plants and flowers, and no longer did the people feel that warmth permeate their bones and lift their spirits. The land was plunged into an eternal winter, and slowly but surely things began to die. Evil lurked in the shadows and the spirits of those who had been cursed walked the earth once more.

"We must do something!" said the god of wisdom, Omoikane. "If we leave things as they are, then we bring chaos to heaven and earth."

He suggested a trick to bring Amaterasu to her senses. The sound of the cock crowing would trigger her memory, and draw her out, for she could not help but perform her daily ritual of rising in the sky. So the gods placed a gaggle of birds outside the cave, but even the sound of their voices would not lure her into the open.

Next, they tried to cajole her with lavish gifts: a beautiful Sakaki tree dripping with sparkling jewels, and a golden mirror, but still she would not budge. Eventually, the goddess of mirth and merry-making Amenouzume took her place outside the entrance, and performed a bawdy dance so ridiculous it made the gods bellow with laughter. They hooted and cried, they whooped and jeered, and the sounds made Amaterasu curious. What could they be doing to make such a cacophony?

Slowly, quietly, she drifted to the cave entrance to take a peek, and it was then that they pulled her out and told her that she could hide no more. They showed her the reflection of her radiant beauty in the golden mirror, they pointed to the valley below and the black cloud that had smothered the land.

In that moment Amaterasu felt her heart swell with love for her people, and she realized just how much they needed her. She drew in a breath with all her might and unleashed a wave of loving energy. Rays of light spilled from every pore, and bathed the earth in warmth as the sun finally began to rise.

Night became day once more, and the people of the Shinto valley rejoiced. The great lady of light was back where she belonged, and she would never hide her shine again.

GODDESS AFFIRMATION
"I am a being of light and love."

GODDESS RITUAL

Amaterasu is a sensitive soul with a generous spirit. She cannot help but shine with love; it is her unique calling and what she was meant to do. Her story shows that we are all unique and have the ability to express ourselves in different ways.

This ritual, which uses the light of the sun to create positive energy, will help to boost self-esteem.

This is best performed first thing in the morning, to help you create a positive mindset for the day.

- Start by throwing the curtains open, so that you can greet the sun.

- Stand with feet hip-width apart, shoulders relaxed.

- Tilt your chin upward, smile and say, "I greet the sun upon its way, it fills me with joy upon this day."

- Take a deep breath and throw your arms wide as if you're going to embrace the sun, then draw them back toward your chest, as if you're pulling the light toward you.

- Exhale, and drop your hands to your sides.

- Imagine that with every inhalation, you're drawing the sun's energizing rays into your chest. With every exhalation, you're sending those rays out into the world.

Chantico

Aztec Goddess of the Hearth and Fire

THEMES
Wisdom, comfort, prosperity, protection

"SHE WHO DWELLS IN THE HOUSE"

Have you ever seen something out of the corner of your eye, a shadow, a flicker, a movement so fast that you wonder if it was ever there in the first place? Magic is like that. It cannot be easily explained, and yet it stays with you—the moment, the imagining, and then you start to ponder. What did it mean, and why was I the one to see it? You muse, and reflect, and wonder if the whole thing was your imagination; because magic is fleeting, especially when it comes from the gods. But it is ever-present too. Sometimes you just don't see it at all unless you really look.

Chantico is like that. She is one of those deities who you can see every day, if you set your mind to it. She's almost a part of the family, and she's certainly central to family life. At least that's what she likes to think, and in ancient times this was more true than ever. Chantico's influence could be felt daily, and because of this, belief in her grew, because when you see something you're more likely to believe in it. So she became a powerful goddess, and not one to be trifled with.

She lives in the heart of the fire. In the burning embers and the towering flames. In the crackle and spit as the wood burns, and the twisting, fiery, flickering dance as it fills the hearth. That is where Chantico makes her home. She is a generous goddess; no half measures with her. If you need her, you simply have to ask, and she will come and fill your home with warmth. In that she is probably more straightforward than all the other Aztec deities, for she does not demand great demonstrations, just an open hearth and a willingness to look into her flames. A guardian spirit, she watches over those who stoke the embers, and even reaches out to them from time to time.

And so she is known as "She who dwells in the house," and her presence is accepted as if she was an elderly auntie, sitting in the corner silently watching and smiling. You can see her, can't you? If you put your mind to it. She is the one with the swarthy golden skin, and the toothy white grin. She rocks back and forth upon her chair in a gradual dance, and while she doesn't demand attention, she likes you to look every now and then to check that she's OK, still alive, and rooted to the spot.

Just like every good elder, she'll be there when you need advice, or just a caring hand upon the shoulder. She'll be there to take your mind off the things that hurt. Whether that's with her warmth or love, or by reminding you that other things hurt more. Yes, she has a sharp tongue and if she does lash out, you'll know it.

But she's seen things in her time, and has made mistakes, so if anyone knows, she does. That's why you should never touch her without asking. If you do, you'll receive a sudden slap, a burning pain to the skin that will surely blister. She once did the same, in her youth. Have you heard the story? She tells it often. She ate some fish covered in paprika, which was banned at the time. But being reckless, she thought she'd get away with it. One of the other gods took offense and turned her into a dog. And that's not something you'd want to happen to you, is it?

Chantico is all about lessons, and learning yours, but if you do, she'll reward you well. She'll nod with pleasure, her crown of poisoned cactus spikes will turn red and she'll shower you with warmth and love, like your favorite auntie. She'll bring you gifts, brightly colored precious stones, tempting dishes hot and steaming from her fires, and warm, soothing drinks. She knows how to get things bubbling and frothy, just how you like them.

You might be forgiven for thinking it's magic, because after all, that's what she is and that's how we started this conversation. But magic can be present all the time. It can live in your home and heart and be a part of every day. It can sit within the hearth like your favorite auntie, cackling and crackling—"She who dwells in the house." All you have to do is look for it.

GODDESS AFFIRMATION

"I am open and ready to learn something new every day."

GODDESS RITUAL

Chantico has a lovely warming energy about her. She likes to be part of family life, to make herself known and then to sit and observe the comings and goings. She is wise and has learned through past mistakes. She knows that every day brings the opportunity to grow and acquire knowledge.

This ritual uses the element of fire to help you grow and attract prosperity in your life.

You will need a fireproof bowl, some paprika, a pen, and some paper.

* Upon the paper write down the things you'd like to attract into your life; these can be qualities, lessons, and also external things. Think in particular about the things you'd like to learn and how they might help you in the future.

* Tear the paper up and drop in the fireproof bowl.

* Sprinkle with a little paprika and say, "By the power of Chantico, I learn, and I grow. I am open and ready for each new day, and all the lessons that come my way."

* Light a match and drop it into the bowl, then watch the paper burn. Notice how the flames grow and dance as they feed on each new lesson.

* To finish, give thanks for the blessings in your life and scatter the ashes away.

Freya

Norse Goddess of Love, Beauty, and War

THEMES
Magnetism, beauty, passion, self-love

"THE GODDESS AND THE BRISINGAMEN"

Imagine if you will a golden-haired goddess, brighter and more beautiful than any before. Her eyes were like the starry ocean, deep blue and glistening. Her lips were like rose petals, and her skin the porcelain white of snow. So gorgeous was she, that men and gods alike fell at her feet. Everyone who encountered her fell in love, but then that's no surprise for she was associated with this, the strongest of emotions. But she was a woman of contradictions, for while she governed love and beauty, she was also a warrior, and made from the strongest of stuff. She could disarm a man with her sword as much as her smile, and this only added to her allure. When she fought, she fought with passion, and as leader of the Valkyries, an all-woman troupe of warriors, she was indestructible. It was their mission to gather the souls of the bravest of warriors and take them to Valhalla, where they would dine in the halls of the gods and celebrate their earthly victories forever.

Being a woman of many different facets, Freya was hard to pin down and while many tried to seduce her with their advances, there were few who gained favor. Those who tried their hand might feel the skin of an axe to their head, or if she was feeling generous, she'd don her feathered cloak, transform into a falcon and fly free of their grasp. That said, there were times when even Freya conceded. The only other thing she collected along with the souls of the dead were pretty gems that she could wear to accentuate her beauty, and for such trinkets she might acquiesce.

And so it was that when Freya was out riding one day upon her chariot, drawn by her two beloved blue-gray cats, she took a detour away from her usual route. She

felt drawn toward the gray mountains and urged her cats onward through the treacherous landscape. Their muscles and claws were well adjusted to deal with such terrain, for they were magical cats, a gift from the god Thor. They thundered up the hillside, leaping from each outcrop, pulling the chariot at speed as Freya pushed them onward.

In truth, she was drawn to the dwelling of four dwarves, for she had heard their names like a whisper on the wind and she felt compelled to visit. Hidden within an enormous slab of rock, their cave was a treasure trove, a forge where they worked tirelessly, crafting jewelry for the gods.

When Freya arrived they were working upon a necklace, an enchanting piece, with a stone at the center that burned like fire. The goddess couldn't take her eyes off it. She had never seen anything quite so dazzling. The gold could have been spun from the nectar of the gods; it held such life and promise that Freya had to have it for herself. For their part, the dwarves were equally as taken with the woman in front of them. They had never seen her in the flesh, and she was indeed a jewel they wished to shape with their own hands.

"Tell me, what is that necklace called? It is so beautiful, I must have it," she said, enraptured.

"The Brisingamen," the four dwarves replied, and added. "It is indeed special, and fit for a goddess."

"What can I give you in return for this piece? I have silver, I have gold, I will give it all to you for that necklace."

The dwarves looked at each other and smiled, for in that moment they knew exactly what they wanted. "There is only one thing we want."

"Tell me," the goddess urged.

"One night with you, one night for each for us, and then the necklace is yours for eternity."

Freya smiled. She could not fault their bravado, and while most would have come to a sticky end had they suggested such a thing, she was indeed taken with the necklace. So for four days and nights the goddess stayed with the dwarves at the forge. What occurred, we shall never know, for Freya was as cunning as she was beautiful, but she was true to her word.

On the fifth day, she departed with her cats in tow. They soared through the air, taking each jagged lip of stone in their enormous stride to return to Asgard. Those who saw them from a distance would have surely noticed the magnificent jewel that shone from Freya's neck. A match for her stunning beauty—it burned like the sun and scattered rays of light upon the earth.

"My natural allure shines through my smile."

GODDESS RITUAL

Freya is not ashamed of her beauty, or her innate sexuality. She embraces it, acknowledges who she is and the passions that stir within her soul. Her lesson is one of self-acceptance and love—the ability to celebrate your natural allure and share this power with the rest of the world.

This ritual works with the stone amber, which is often associated with the power of the Brisingamen. It can help to boost confidence and self-love.

You'll need a piece of amber and a candle.

* Light the candle and place the amber in front of it.

* Gaze at the flame and breathe deeply for a couple of minutes. Imagine taking the light of the fire into your soul with every breath.

* Pick up the amber and hold it over your throat chakra, which is situated at the base of the throat, in the center.

* Picture golden rays of light streaming from the stone, into your throat, and down into your chest.

* Feel the warm energy fill you up with confidence and love.

* Say, "I draw on the power of this gem to fill my heart with love. To help me see my beauty and feel blessings from above."

* Place the amber beneath your pillow every night and repeat the magical chant to help focus your mind, boost self-esteem, and imbue your subconscious with positive energy.

Hel

Norse Goddess of Death and the Underworld

THEMES
Transition, personal power, reflection, strength

"FALL TO THE UNDERWORLD"

In the deepest, darkest recesses, beneath the earth's surface, there resides a place of torment. It is a place where the dead wander, their souls in turmoil. It is a land known as the World of Darkness, given the same name as its queen, and that name is Hel. To enter this space you must first encounter the hound of hell, hear its blood-curdling wail, then pass through the cave into the inner sanctum. Here you will find desperation and despair go hand in hand. The air is thick with the dust of the dead, and their bodies litter the shoreline. This is not a place that people seek out freely and nor should they if they value their peace.

Hel is a giantess, and the daughter of the trickster god Loki, so you might expect that she would be different from the rest of the deities. Some even say she is only half a god, or mostly human, but it is her birthright that gives her power and meaning. Perhaps that is why she was so despised by the great father Odin and why he ultimately cast her into the ether, tipping her over the edge of Asgard, where the gods of the Aesir reside.

Down and down she fell. She plunged through the atmosphere, the layers of existence, stripping her of all humanity until what was left was a half being, her face split between startling beauty on the one side and that of a spectral corpse on the other. Finally she found her feet, landing beyond the world of men and into the shadowy deep. While most would have crumbled, letting the darkness swallow them whole, Hel was not one to give up. Dusting herself down and drawing a breath, she smiled. She would prove her worth.

"So this is where I find myself." She gazed about her, probing the depths, and reaching out with her mind.

"Then this is where I shall make my home, and it will be called Hel like me, and here I will be queen." She grinned and threw her arms in the air. "This Underworld is mine, and those who wish to enter bow to me, for I am the divine and death will be the fee!" True to her word, for her word was the law in this domain, Hel became the goddess of the Underworld and she ruled from her castle in the north. Filled with the venom of a host of serpents, it was a place where the darkest of souls would go. A place for murderers to languish, while the great dragon Nidhogg sucked the blood from their bodies, leaving them pallid and broken.

Most who found themselves in the Underworld deserved to be there, but there is always one who breaks the rules. When Hel's father Loki slayed the beloved god Baldur, his spirit went to Hel, though having such a bright light in such a murky place did not sit well with the other deities.

Hel on the other hand was delighted at her new arrival. It was a boon to have such a prominent and well-liked god among the sniveling wretches of the dead, and it gave her a degree of power.

The deities decided to send an emissary Hermod to retrieve Baldur from her realm, but the visit did not go well. Hel agreed only to give up his soul if every living thing in the world openly wept for him. And it seemed that the task was almost achieved, for Baldur was cherished by gods and mortals. Even the stars in the sky and the birds and animals adored him. But there was one who would never weep for his soul, and that was the giantess Thokk, who many believed was Loki in disguise.

"A deal, is a deal," she told Hermod sweetly, "and while he may have almost everyone breaking their heart at his sudden demise, it seems there is a giantess who does not weep, and so that means his soul I keep."

And so it was that Baldur remained in the deep and gloomy Underworld and for the first time since being cast out by the gods, by those who should have been her family, Hel had won. She had proved that she was indeed a worthy goddess. She had made her mark in the Underworld, made it her domain, and it would remain that way till the end of the days when the gods of Aesir finally fell.

Hel

"Each challenge is an opportunity to grow and step into my power."

GODDESS RITUAL

Hel is often misunderstood. While she is a goddess of death, she is also about transition and having the courage to face your fear and evolve. She resides over the darkness and urges us to reflect and look within our own dark spaces.

Hel is often depicted with half her face black and half white, to represent the darkness and the light, and also the fact that she is half dead. While these two shades are opposites, together they create balance and wholeness.

This ritual uses the power of light and dark to help you identify areas for growth and change.

You'll need a black candle and a white candle of roughly the same size and shape, a sheet of paper, and a pen.

* To start, stand the candles side by side and light them.

* Take the paper and draw a line down the center.

* Make a list down one side of all your positive traits, and on the other side make a list of what you consider to be negative traits.

* Look at both sides and notice if they're equal in size. Is one side bigger than the other? If so, why?

* Are there things you can do to make this more balanced, or so that you have more traits on the positive side?

* Next, consider the negative traits, and how you can learn from them. Perhaps they are not as negative as you first think, and you can use them in a different way. For example, if you think that you nitpick faults, then perhaps you can use this skill in a more analytical way to help others.

* To finish, read all the positive traits. Remember that you are a balance of both sides, and that is what makes you unique and wonderful.

Water, Sea, and Moon

From turning the tides of fate to turning the tides of the ocean, the deities within this section embrace the element of water in some form. There are those who govern the emotions, and know how to let love flow, and those who show their adoration by lighting up the night sky with their gentle luminescence. You'll find goddesses of the rivers and the sea, and those who helped to shape the world by simply letting it rain.

One thing's certain, water is an unstoppable force, and these ladies use this to their advantage. Be prepared for passion and compassion in equal measure, dalliances between moon and earth, and salty sea creatures who protect the ocean deep, not to mention those magical types who simply like to come out when the moon is high in the sky. Then there's the resilient ones, who crave the icy cold kiss of a frozen stream as much as their dream guy.

These goddesses encourage you to stretch your imagination, to release the past, and let it go. Whatever floats your boat and gets you jumping in feet first, they urge you to do you, to follow your heart's desire.

Yemaya

Yoruban Goddess of the Ocean

THEMES
Wisdom, endurance, inner strength, calm

"MAMI WATA"

There was once a girl, a little lost girl, who wandered too close to the ocean. Like lots of young girls her age, she was feeling confused. Blossoming womanhood, and all the things that this brought with it, were spinning around in her head. She longed for some peace, to quell the waters deep within, and calm her mind by gazing at the sea. And so, when no one was looking, she walked toward the water's edge and traced a path along the shoreline. Deep in thought, she paid little attention to where she was going. It was more important to be beside the sea, to drink in the ocean, and to share her problems by casting them like pebbles into the waves. When she realized that she had walked too far, and could not see her family or friends, she stopped, took a breath, and looked out at Mami Wata.

For while the girl was foolish to have wandered far, she was not alone. As a child she'd been told tales of the Queen of the Sea, of the great goddess Yemaya, and how she gave birth to all the rivers and the ocean when her waters broke in childbirth. She'd heard the tales of how Yemaya had crafted the earth and gave life to the fish that filled the seven seas. She knew of the Mother of All, she felt a connection to her, and, most importantly, she knew Mami Wata would always come to her aid. So instead of crying out or panicking, she looked out toward the middle of the ocean and said, "Mami, come show me the way for I need your guidance right now."

When the girl looked, she could see a ring of white froth the color of the moon, and ripples forming around it. The sea was stirring, and something was moving to the surface. Slowly and elegantly, Mami Wata rose, a vision in blue, all lithe and graceful with her mermaid tail.

"What do you have for me, little one?" she cried.

The girl stepped forward, and produced a silvery cowrie shell, which she cast into the water.

"I am lost, Mami. I need guidance, can you help me?"

Yemaya, goddess and Queen of the Sea, smiled.

"Child, that is what I am here for," and she beckoned her closer.

The girl stepped toward the shoreline, then tentatively dipped her toe in.

Mami Wata watched, and stretched out her arms urging her onward.

"Come child, come into my arms," she cajoled, and the girl strode into the ocean, one foot in front of the other until her skirts were wet, and the waves were rising above her waist.

"But Mami, I am scared," she whispered.

"Don't be, I am here, and I will not leave you." She stretched out her arms even further, and soon her fingertips were reaching for the girl's hands, tugging her toward the center of the sea.

If you or I had been watching, we might have thought that she was going for a swim, and that she had swam too far and lost control; that the ocean was about to drag her under, and that would be the end of that. Except that Yemaya is not a cruel goddess by choice. She is a mother first and foremost, and her role is to offer salvation, to navigate, and guide her charges.

Sometimes she forgets herself because she loves humankind so much, particularly the female of the species, and like any mother she wants to keep them close. In doing so she forgets that they cannot breathe beneath her waters. But this is not one of those times. This time, she leads her daughter through the rippling rolling ocean, and out toward the other side. She shows her the way, and as the girl swims, she learns that she can embrace life and go with the flow. She can ride the waves and sometimes go under, without completely losing herself. She has more control than she thinks and, like any fish, she can carve a path and find a new direction.

And when she emerges from the ocean, soaked to the skin, the girl feels refreshed, recharged, and ready for anything. She has found her way back to her family and friends, but more than that, she has found her way back to herself.

From somewhere deep beneath the tumbling waves, Mami Wata smiles. She twists and turns, watching her mermaid tail glint turquoise and blue, and in her hands she holds a silvery cowrie shell, a gift from one of her thousands of children.

"Calmness flows over me and soothes my soul."

GODDESS RITUAL

Yemaya, also known as Mami Wata, is the beautiful and wise Yoruban goddess of the ocean. Protective and loving, she can also take away what she has given. She offers guidance and healing and shows her followers that they can navigate rough waters and emerge from turbulent times stronger than ever.

This ritual, which uses one of Yemaya's symbols, a seashell, will help you connect with the healing element of water and tap into your inner wisdom.

You'll need a shell and a glass of water, plus a notebook to record your thoughts.

✳ Pour a glass of chilled water and place the shell in front of it.

✳ Say, "Let this water I sip refresh and heal my body, mind and soul." Then slowly sip the water while letting any thoughts come and go. Try not to hold on to any worries; just breathe, sip, and connect with the element of water.

✳ When you're ready, hold the shell in both hands and close your eyes. Imagine you are beside the sea and breathe in that tranquility.

✳ Say, "This gift of the sea brings me closer to the ocean deep, and the wisdom held within."

✳ Lift the shell to your ear, relax, and listen. It doesn't matter if you don't hear anything, just breathe, and let your intuition rise up. You might experience emotions, a vision, or just a prominent thought that holds some significance.

✳ When you're ready, open your eyes and write any thoughts in your notebook.

✳ Keep the shell with you, to strengthen your connection with the healing element of water.

Selene

Greek Goddess of the Moon

THEMES
Love, illumination, imagination, connection

"A NEVER-ENDING LOVE STORY"

As the sun begins to set, swooping like a diving bird toward the land, a silence settles upon the earth. It is a moment of respite, a time for stillness to take control of the conscious mind. Those who have long been awake will find themselves drifting into a dream, and those who sleep might stir from their slumber, but there is one dreamer who will never awaken. He has chosen to sleep the eternal sleep in his cave high up in the mountains.

His name is Endymion, the shepherd prince and grandson of the great god Zeus, and he is the most beautiful man upon the earth. Why he chose this state of being, no one knows. Some believe it was a gift bestowed by his grandfather, a reward, and a way to retain his beauty. Others believe it to be a curse, a punishment for some earthly evil doing. The truth remains a mystery and matters little in this tale.

Being fair of face, he has caught the attention of many over the years, but there is one whose heart beats only for him; a heavenly consort, and a goddess. She watches over him nightly, and her passion grows. Her name is Selene. Serene and glowing, she is the Greek goddess of the moon. While she has had many lovers over many lifetimes, for who wouldn't want to spend time basking in her glory, Endymion is the only one who touches her soul with such grace. He is different from all the rest. He pulls her to him with every sleeping breath and she longs to reach out, to touch his face with more than just her spectral fingers.

In her heart she knows that this love is one-sided, for how can she truly understand him in this half state, and yet she cannot forget him. The memory of his face seeps beneath her translucent skin and her gaze is drawn once more to the cave. This is the story that plagues her every

night; this is her destiny. A chaste glimpse is never going to be enough for a goddess of the moon, and Selene is more mighty than most, for she has the power to suspend time and dance across the sky. She has the ability to see into the hearts and minds of men, to illuminate the darkest parts, and bring to light and life the goodness within. She is a moon goddess who truly cares about her people and wants to connect with them at a deeper level.

And so it is that the moon will not simply hang in the sky, watching and waiting for her love to stir. No, she will move heaven and earth to be at his side, to be close and share her comfort.

She will shift shape and form over the days of each month.

She will transform and cast her light, farther than ever before.

She will ride her chariot through the sky, her gleaming robes flowing behind her as she gallops onward.

Eventually she will reach the cave where Endymion sleeps, forever youthful, but motionless and lost in a dream. There she will encase him in the luminescence of her love. She will rest in his arms, and in return he will give her a child, a daughter to represent each of the fifty lunar months of the Olympiad.

And so it goes on, and on.

You might think this is a strange love story, one with no clear beginning or end, but then the cycles of the moon are like that—they merge together to create one long, lingering existence.

Whether Endymion is ever aware of her presence, it is hard to tell, for like so many things, the moon's light is subtle and ethereal. She does not seek to blind those who step into her orbit. She only wishes to share a little love, and brightness, to lift the spirits and stimulate the imagination.

Whether you're a hopeless dreamer, a born romantic, or someone seeking solace, Selene offers peace, purity, and the promise of enlightenment. She is there in the in-between as you drift into a dream. She is there while you sleep, even though you cannot see her.

She is a never-ending love story.

"I connect with my heart and mind, and let the gentle light of illumination fill me with love."

GODDESS RITUAL

Selene is a goddess who likes to share her light and love with everyone. While she feels things deeply, she is not overly pushy or controlling. She prefers to take the gentle approach, adapting to the situation and being kind to herself and others.

This ritual will help you to become an emotional shapeshifter. You'll learn how to connect and respond to the energy of others and open your heart to the flow of love.

* Start by spending some time basking beneath the glow of the moon. Simply stand outside, or near a window where you can see the night sky. Focus on the moon for a few minutes, then close your eyes and imagine that with every breath, you draw in the light of the moon.

* Feel the soft glow permeate your being until you feel totally relaxed. Continue to breathe and enjoy those feelings.

* Whenever you wish to connect with someone at a deeper level, draw your attention to the center of your chest.

* Remember how the light of the moon made you feel calm and peaceful. Conjure this energy by picturing a small full moon sitting in the middle of your chest.

* Draw a long breath in and every time you exhale, feel the light of the moon extending outward, until eventually it bathes everyone near you in its gentle glow.

* Continue to breathe deeply and ask Selene to help you connect with others from the heart.

* In your mind, say, "I let the flow of love pass between us, illuminating our thoughts and filling us with joyful energy."

Jaci

Brazilian Moon Goddess

THEMES
Stillness, peace,
healing, nature

"A BEACON OF HOPE"

Damp and dark lays the blanket of the Amazon at night. Thick with shadows, and the soft pawing sound of the jaguar as he makes his way through the forest bed. Humming, thrumming noises fill the air as the creatures stir, for they know this is their home. It is an ethereal place, a realm of enchantment, and it is thanks to the soft glow of the moon's charms, which lifts the atmosphere. Like a gentle melody, she accentuates the shapes and adds depth and lightness to the vista. She is a beacon of hope for all who wander in these parts.

It hasn't always been this way. At the dawn of time, the people were plunged into a darkness as black as obsidian. The night was oppressive, especially after the dazzling beauty of the sun, but he was long since gone to his bed and deep in slumber.

And while humankind struggled to see and breathe as day slipped away, the deities, too, were suffering. For them the night was a hungry mouth ready to swallow up their powers.

"This cannot go on," said the thunder god, Tupã. "When Guaraci the sun god sleeps, it is as if the world ends, and he takes all the light with him." It was then that he had an idea. He would fashion a new deity, a goddess so beautiful and bright that she could illuminate the darkest sky, and be a beacon of hope for humans and gods alike.

"Her skin will shine as if it was lit up from the inside, and her eyes will shimmer like stars. When she takes her position in the heavens no one will be able to take their eyes off her; she will be stunning." And so Tupã created the moon goddess Jaci and, just as he had said, she was the most magnificent being who had ever existed. Her movements were like liquid, like a trickle of water

from a mountain stream, and her smile was vibrant, like the many plants and flowers that grew in the rainforest. Her heart was open and filled with love for her surroundings, and in that instant she became Jaci, the protectress of plants and animals, governed by the element of water.

When Guaraci awoke from his dreaming, he was so taken aback by her beauty, he could hardly breathe. Love flowed from him in a wave of blinding sunshine.

It burned a path through the trees and lit up the sky, but more than that, it became so hot that the earth began to crumble. His ardor blazed a trail through the forest, and as his infatuation grew, so, too did the amount of destruction that he caused.

Jaci, for her part, was also enamored. She could see herself reflected in the sun god's rays, and she longed to be in his embrace, but she could also see the devastation that this passion between them had caused.

She cried then, for the last thing she wanted to do was cause harm to her people, and as her tears fell they put out the fires and the land was once more quenched.

Taking a moment to still her beating heart, she came to a decision.

"We cannot be together," she told Guaraci, "for our love, though it is deep, is also destructive and we would destroy the world. We must ensure that we are forever apart, that when you arise from your bed I will go to mine, and when the day is over and you are done, that is when I will take my place in the sky."

Guaraci was heartbroken, but he agreed that this was the only way they could both exist, apart from those stolen seconds that happened from time to time, when the sun and moon would join in an eclipse.

"I will forever watch you, and wait for the moment when our paths cross, and that will have to be enough to sustain me."

That night, as Jaci slipped out of the shadows to take her position, her heart was so full of woe that she thought it might shatter to pieces. The pain was such that all she could do was wail and let the tears come once more, this time in a great flood of emotion. As the grief poured out of her, it hit the earth, forming a giant pool, which swelled to become the River Amazon.

From that moment on, the lovers were always apart, slipping past each other to take their turn in the sky. Never once did they complain—they played their role in the cosmic dance—the sun with its life-giving power, and the moon, a beacon of hope for all.

"I take the time to be still and calm my soul."

GODDESS RITUAL

Jaci has a beautiful heart. She is a gentle, caring goddess, who does all she can to create a peaceful home for her people. She knows that moments of stillness are what everyone needs to heal and renew. She also knows that there is no need to seek attention; simply being yourself is enough to captivate the entire world.

This ritual, which works with the element of water, will help you find inner peace and restore your soul.

You will need some sandalwood essential oil, and a bath.

* Start by running yourself a bath and add in four or five drops of the essential oil. Inhale the musky, sweet aroma as the bath fills.

* When you have enough water, climb in and simply relax. Close your eyes and soak in the water.

* Take long, deep breaths, and drink in the fragrance.

* As you exhale, imagine that you are releasing any negative energy from your body.

* As you relax, notice how the water feels against your skin. Also notice how the gentle warmth is nurturing, just like the light of the moon.

* Picture yourself floating in the tropical waters of the rainforest. Look up and see the light of the moon bathing you in her healing rays.

* Breathe and take in the calming energy of your surroundings.

* Hold on to this moment of stillness, and keep it with you every day, by inhaling the essential oil and taking some time to recreate the image of the rainforest in your mind.

Green Tara

Buddhist Goddess of Enlightenment and Compassion

THEMES
Generosity, compassion, enlightenment, accomplishment

"THE ENLIGHTENED ONE"

In the early days, when the earth was still finding its feet and humans were learning the ways of the land, help was needed to alleviate the suffering. The souls of men and women were in torment, for life was fraught with trials and tribulations. Simply being in control of the emotions was a hero's task, and every day there was something new to learn. Humankind struggled to find their way spiritually and physically because the world was littered with challenges. Evil lurked in the shadows, looking for a way in, an opening from which to contort innocent souls.

The great bodhisattva of infinite compassion and wisdom, Avalokiteshvara, worked tirelessly to help those who were floundering. Applying all the knowledge he had accumulated to lead them to enlightenment, he did his utmost, but the world was enormous and it was a thankless task, even for one as accomplished as he. It mattered not how much effort he put in, for the people were still in anguish, and it seemed there was no light at the end of the tunnel.

Avalokiteshvara's heart broke at the thought that he could not help, and as that realization settled within, he began to cry. At first his tears were a gentle trickle, but soon they were streaming down his cheeks, and he was sobbing with such force that a puddle began to form at his feet. Slowly, gradually, it became a pool of water that spread into a stream and then a glistening silver lake.

He watched as the water swirled and he wondered there and then what he had created.

"What is the meaning of this?" he pondered.

Then, as if in answer, the lake began to stir, and ripples formed at the center that expanded outward, and it

reminded him of acts of kindness and how these can spread from one to another. And as Avalokiteshvara's mind contemplated the sight in front of him, the water began to part, and a lotus emerged from the shimmering depths. The flower began to grow, the delicate petals stretching upward, and then eventually opening to reveal a woman standing at its heart. Her skin, though white upon first glance, also looked green, exposing the two aspects of her personality. She stared at Avalokiteshvara, and there was such understanding and compassion in that one moment that he knew straight away her true purpose.

"I am Tara," she said, and her voice was like birdsong; each word danced before his eyes and filled him with hope.

She stepped from the lotus onto dry land and wrapped her arms around his neck. She wiped away his tears with her hair and sang the sweetest lullaby to ease the ache within.

"I am here to help you with this mammoth task. Together we *will* free all beings from suffering and bring enlightenment. As Green Tara, I represent the night; I am like the half-open lotus. I am the embodiment of enlightened activity." She positioned herself at his side, her left leg folded, her right extended outward, ready to leap into action if required. Then as if to demonstrate the difference, she moved into the diamond lotus position, with the soles of her feet pointing upward.

"And this is me as White Tara. In this guise I represent the day, and the lotus fully open. I am the embodiment of grace and serenity. In both of these forms I can reach out and show humankind the way to enlightenment. I will protect them from evil and give my love generously." But while Green and White Tara were one and the same, they could not reside upon the land, such was their power, and if they were truly to show the way, they needed an exalted position from which to do that. So Green Tara became the North Star in the sky, and a leading light for those on the earth. Whenever a person had lost their way, all they had to do was gaze up at the night sky and they would see her watching over them.

As she was a being of great compassion, she shone more brightly than the other stars, and her light was such that she had the power to touch the soul and lift the spirits. All of humankind benefited from her benevolence, and though the world was still littered with challenges, the highs and lows were easier to navigate with the enlightened one's help.

"When I act with kindness, I am filled with joy."

GODDESS RITUAL

Green Tara is one aspect of the goddess Tara that represents enlightened activity, so while she is all about finding the stillness within, she is far from passive. Tara acts when she sees someone in need. She goes out of her way to connect and empathize. She is a force of nature, and kindness is at the heart of everything she does.

This ritual, which features the power of the stars, helps you develop empathy for others and yourself.

It is best performed in the evening when you can clearly see the stars in the sky for inspiration.

- Go outside on a starry night. If you have an outdoor space, you might want to lie down on a blanket looking up at the stars, or simply stand or sit beneath the sky.

- Spend a few minutes breathing deeply to calm your body and mind.

- Gaze up at the heavens and look at the stars. You'll probably find that one shines brighter than the others, but as you continue to study the sky, you'll notice others emerge. Soon, you'll make out a pattern of stars.

- Notice the pictures they make in the sky and see if you can pick out some of the more obvious constellations.

- Notice, too, how these stars are connected and create a beautiful starry collage in the sky, just as we are all connected upon the earth and when we come together, we, too, create magic.

- Close your eyes and imagine the blanket of stars wrapping around you. Feel the light of the stars fill you with vibrant, loving energy.

- To finish, think of the network of stars in your orbit: your family and friends, neighbors, and people in your community, and how you can reach out to them and make those connections stronger and brighter.

Chalchiuhtlicue

Aztec Goddess of the River and Sea

THEMES
Emotional honesty, self-expression, self-acceptance, fertility

"WHEN WE WERE FISH"

When the Aztec deities created the world, they wanted it to be perfect, so much so that they tried five times to get it right. While each time was special and sacred, there was always a reason why each world wasn't right and would have to be created again. By the fourth attempt, they were fairly certain that all was as it should be. After all, they'd had plenty of practice and, to be fair, the gods must surely have been running out of steam. It takes a lot of time and energy to make a planet, nevermind the entire universe and everything above and below. And so once more the world was born, and with it a new sun.

Each world needed a sun for light, energy, and warmth, and the fourth sun was just as bright and powerful as all the rest; in fact probably more so, because it was governed by the goddess Chalchiuhtlicue. You might think this was rather strange, since she was not a fire deity; her element was water, and she ruled the rivers and seas. Even so, she was given this responsibility and, being a conscientious goddess, she took it very seriously.

For the most part Chalchiuhtlicue cared deeply about the people of the earth and gave freely of her gifts. She wandered the heavens, "she of the jade skirt," and when she danced the showers fell. She watered the land and ensured that their crops grew in abundance, she filled their rivers and streams with drinking water and fish, and when they asked, and petitioned her with worship and offerings, she was only too happy to shake her skirts and let the rain fall even more.

But of course, like any of us (and the deities are more like us than we might imagine) she had bad days. Sometimes it was her husband the rain god, Tlaloc, who

made her grumpy. Sometimes it was the other deities, believing they were far superior and making it known, who made her angry, and sometimes it was just because she felt out of sorts. On one of those days you could expect more than your fair share of rain. It would be true to say that when Chalchiuhtlicue was enraged, she was like a bear with a sore head. The sky would darken and split in two, and her wrath would come down in waves that flooded the land.

So while she could give, she could also take away, making her somewhat unpredictable and governed by her emotions. That said, she ruled the fourth sun and provided plentiful water for her people for 676 years, which is quite some feat, and also quite specific! Her reign would have continued, too, had it not been for Tezcatlipoca. He was the god of the first sun and an embittered character. In truth, he was unhappy that he no longer played a role in the comings and goings of the world, and he was jealous of the love that Chalchiuhtlicue showed those on earth. For many years he'd remained silent, but no longer could he contain his envy, and in a fit of rage he accused her of being insincere. "You do not really love your people; you're doing it all for the power!" he snapped.

Now, you or I might have stood our ground if someone accused us of being superficial, but Chalchiuhtlicue was a sensitive soul and his words cut deep. Overcome with emotion, she began to cry. And she continued to cry, great, gushing rivers of tears, for fifty-two years. Now that's a lot of water!

Not once did she allow her sun to shine and evaporate any of the tears she'd cried, and not once did she stop for breath. So the inevitable happened; after all that time and weeping, the earth eventually drowned. The people turned into fish, the land was swallowed, and those who did not adapt, died. The heavens collapsed, and the fourth world was destroyed. End of story.

But before you make a judgment on Chalchiuhtlicue, it is worth mentioning this. If it hadn't been for her reaction and what followed, then the fifth world, the one that you and I exist in, wouldn't have been born. The Aztec gods might never have got it right. The earth as it is today would be gone, and we would all be fish.

"I express myself with honesty and integrity."

GODDESS RITUAL

Chalchiuhtlicue is in touch with her emotions. While she might come across as sensitive, she is open and expresses how she feels, which ultimately leads to a better world for everyone. She is a model of self-acceptance, and doesn't try to change who she is; she simply tries to be the best version of herself.

This ritual uses the element of water to help you express any emotions that you have been holding on to, so that you can feel light, bright, and happy with who you are.

You'll need to visit a free-flowing body of water, so this could be the sea, a river, a stream, or a creek. You'll also need a white flower to symbolize purity and the emotions you wish to express.

✳ Stand before the water, holding the flower head in your hands.

✳ Think about the emotions that you'd like to get off your chest; bring them to the forefront of your heart and mind.

✳ If there's something you want to say, say it out loud or in your head.

✳ Imagine pouring all of those feelings into the flower. Don't be shy, this is your chance to express how you truly feel and to release it.

✳ When you're ready, throw the flower into the water and say, "I release these emotions, I let them flow. I express myself, I let it go."

✳ Watch the flower drift away, and know that you have opened your heart, and been true to yourself. You should feel a sense of peace at letting your true feelings flow.

Artemis

Greek Goddess of Wild Animals, the Hunt, and the Moon

THEMES
Freedom, self-respect, patience, personal power

"SHE OF THE WILD"

She runs through the woods, as fast as a deer. Her hair streams in ribbons behind her, her legs push forward, bow and arrow in hand. She is primed and ready for whatever comes her way, for while she may look like a huntress, and indeed she is more skilled than most, her role is that of protector. She is strength dressed up in a delicate form, with her tunic skimming her knees, and a crown the shape of a crescent moon upon her head. You know straight away there is something different about her. Her skin shines with luminescence, a heavenly gift from the moon that fuels her power and strength. She has animal instincts, senses so alive she can spy the tiniest being in a cluster of trees, and hear the slightest shuffle or snuffle among the leaves, and at night the moon lights her path, showing her the way and igniting her intuition.

While she can hunt, she does not do so for sport. To her the animals of the forest are her kin, and anyone who treats them with disrespect is sure to feel her wrath. She is chaste, too, a virgin goddess, who is proud of her status and does not swoon at the sight of a handsome man. Humans offer little to excite her; she gets her kicks roaming the undergrowth and climbing trees. That said, if there were one to turn her head it would be Orion the hunter, for he understands her calling, and could almost be her equal.

They call her the "mistress of animals" and the "torch-bringer," a nod to her link to the moon and its influence upon her, but she casts light in many different ways, just as the lunar orb changes its shape and form. Should she cross your path, for you will never be able to cross hers unharmed, she may choose to share her brightness, but only if you treat her with respect. Just as she campaigns

for the same for the creatures of the forest, she demands it from you. Do not look her in the eye with attitude unless you want to feel the quiver of her arrow, or the blunt edge of her dagger. And never, ever spy upon her.

To that end, you will most certainly suffer, just as her hunting companion Actaeon did. You could say he was young and foolish, but he knew the score, and he also knew that there was one thing Artemis cherished almost as much as her beloved animals, and that was her chastity. They had been hunting together many times, sharing the spoils to feed their people. They were, by all accounts, friends.

Then one fateful day, while wandering through the woods in search of her, Actaeon crossed a line. Whether she knew he was coming or not is another matter. The boy should have been more cautious. Instead he stole his way through the trees to her favorite bathing spot, a sacred spring in honor of her beauty. From a distance he could see that she was there, he could see her naked form and, instead of turning away, or better still, making a hasty retreat, he crept forward. His belly low to the ground, in stealthy hunting mode, he moved slowly so as not to alert her to his presence. But what Actaeon seemed to have forgotten in a moment of youthful lust was that Artemis was a hunter too, the best in both the heavens and the earthly realm, and she already knew he was there.

Bent low, he moved with grace, getting closer and closer to get a better view of her naked form, when from out of the blue she struck. And while it could have been a fatal blow because Artemis never misses with an arrow, it was more deadly. She reached out with her powers and in one swift flick of the hand she transformed him into a stag.

For a moment he stood, disbelieving at what had happened. Then he heard his own hunting dogs in the distance. They were running at speed, heading in his direction. There was only one thing he could do, and that was to leap into action himself. The chase was on, and although Actaeon had a headstart, it did not end well for him when the dogs finally caught up.

Cruel, perhaps. Necessary, yes, for Artemis the virgin goddess will never let any man take her honor or darken her reputation.

She is of the wild, and she runs free, and *no one* will ever tame her.

"Freedom is my choice, my right, and my power."

GODDESS RITUAL

Artemis is a powerful and popular goddess. Her strength of will, and her dexterity mean she is admired by gods and humans alike; she defiantly protects wild animals, and also her freedom to choose her destiny. Her lesson is one of self-respect and personal power.

This ritual, which connects with the crescent moon, will help you step into your personal power and run free.

You will need a sheet of paper, a pen, and a white candle.

* Start by lighting the candle and spend some time focusing on the flame. Let it calm your mind and settle your thoughts as you gaze at it.

* When you feel centered, take the paper, and draw a large crescent moon facing upward. This is one of the symbols of Artemis, and she is often depicted wearing it as a crown.

* Imagine this is your crown, and when you wear it on your head it accentuates your skills and qualities.

* Next think about those skills, qualities, and strengths that you'd like to build upon and write them in or along the crescent moon shape that you have drawn.

* Close your eyes and bring your attention to the top of your head.

* Picture a crescent moon resting there. Just like the one you have drawn, it embodies all the attributes you have listed.

* Feel it sitting there, imbuing you with power.

* To finish, say, "I am powerful, I am capable, I am free."

* Position the crescent moon sketch somewhere that you can see it every day and be reminded of your magnificence.

Arianrhod

Celtic Goddess of the Moon and the Silver Wheel

THEMES
Time, fate,
rebirth, manifestation

"THE SILVER WHEEL"

In a place between time and space, somewhere beyond the moon's luminescent shadow, there was a palace made of light known as Caer Arianrhod. It stood upon a revolving island, an ethereal land nestled somewhere among the stars—impossible to see with the naked eye or any other instrument, because it was magic.

Made from the glistening tears of the great mother goddess Don, it shone like a spider's web in the sun, and housed a million rooms. You might be wondering why such a palace existed; after all, what is the point if you cannot behold its beauty? But this place was different. It moved and changed with the gifted souls who inhabited its corridors. It was a sacred space, a place where the dead could reside before taking the arduous journey to their final destination. It was also the home of the stunning moon goddess Arianrhod.

Also born from the Celtic goddess Don, this cosmic enchantress held the fates of many in her hands. A skilled weaver, she governed the Silver Wheel, which steadily turned to determine destiny. Each spin brought something different to the lives of those it controlled. It was a huge responsibility, and one that Arianrhod took seriously, for while she cast the threads of change upon the earth she also took the reins in death, gathering the souls of those who had passed upon her ship, the Oar Wheel, and transporting them to the Moonland. There she would judge their deeds and misdeeds and decide upon their resting place.

You might know her island better as the Otherworld, a place between this world and the next, a stepping stone and a space that you can easily slip into once you've entered the dream state. You may even have been there,

although you'd never know. To you it was a dream, a surreal notion that comes to you in broken fragments in the daylight.

While Arianrhod nurtured and loved her people and cared deeply about the twists and turns of their lives, she also had a passion for the sea, and a weakness for mermen. She loved nothing more than to descend into the ocean and indulge her senses. Such recklessness was to be her undoing, for while she could control the lives of others, her own threads were indeed unraveling.

Her uncle Math had been placed under a curious curse, which meant that whenever he refrained from battle, he should rest his feet in the lap of a virgin. Gwydion, his magical successor, suggested Arianrhod for the role, after she spurned his advances. Being both dutiful and independent she accepted, for in her mind, it would be better to play this role than be Gwydion's wife. However the proposal was nothing more than a cheap trick to humiliate the goddess.

On arrival at King Math's palace, Arianrhod had to prove her worth and virginity by stepping over a magical rod. For once, the tables were turned and the Silver Wheel was to determine her fate. Believing she was pure, she strode over the rod confidently, only to be struck down with crippling pain. Gripping her sides, and rocking forward, the goddess gave birth to twins. One was fair of face and a child of the sea named Dylan, who fled to the ocean to be with his merman father. The other was a cruel disfigurement, made mostly of afterbirth. He was whisked away by the cunning Gwydion and raised in a magical forest.

And so it was that Arianrhod became something of a laughing stock among her peers, or at least that's how she felt, and some might say the story ends this way. Except that this is a goddess of time and fate, a powerful weaver who has the ability to create new strands of life from the stars in the sky, and she would not be defeated in this way.

Following her calling, she returned to Caer Arianrhod to consider the measure of her ways and it gave her new insight into the cycles of life, and how they flow. She began to weave a new web with the Silver Wheel within her grasp, and she emerged with a renewed sense of peace. For time is endless, like Arianrhod's wheel. It moves in a continual loop, offering rebirth with every spin, whether you are human or a goddess.

So the next time you gaze up at the stars, or drift into a dream that carries you farther than the moon, remember the

Silver Wheel that is within your grasp. Remember, too, that like Arianrhod, you have the power to weave your own fate, and create a reality made of stars.

GODDESS AFFIRMATION
"My thoughts manifest my reality."

GODDESS RITUAL

Arianrhod's story is a good representation of the cycles of life. There are highs and lows, but just like this goddess, we have the ability to create our reality. A nurturing deity, Arianrhod is governed by her emotions, and always follows her heart. She illustrates that while we cannot control destiny, we must always be true to ourselves.

This ritual, which uses the power of your mind, will help you take control of your reality and manifest a joyful outcome. Set some time aside so that you don't have to rush the process.

✳ Find a quiet, comfortable space where you won't be disturbed.

✳ Think about your reality, and how you'd like to feel. For example, perhaps you want to feel calm and grounded.

✳ Now challenge yourself to think of a scenario where you would feel this way, for example sitting on the beach, watching the gentle lap of the waves at the shore.

✳ Close your eyes and take yourself to this place. Conjure the scene in your mind, and engage all of your senses; think about what you can see, hear, smell, taste, and touch.

✳ Spend a few minutes bringing this image to life. Relax and breathe.

✳ Say, "I carry this feeling with me today, no matter how the Silver Wheel spins, this is me." Whenever you need to create this feeling, simply bring the image to mind and relax.

Skadi

THEMES
Freedom, courage,
resilience, truth

**"THE GIRL WHO ROSE
LIKE A MOUNTAIN"**

At the heart of the harshest winter, when the snow forms a thick and icy crust that swallows everything, and the cold gnaws savagely at your bones, there you will find the Norse goddess Skadi.

When the blizzard steals your sight, and you are lost in a snowstorm, numb, shivering, and wondering at your own mortality, then the giantess will come. She will stride in her enormous snowshoes, splitting the vista in two and making short work of anything in her way.

For it is among the mountains, in the bleakest of conditions, that Skadi finds her home. Others might have perished, were they left to their own devices in such a place, but she is not like any other deity. Skadi is fearless, although she hasn't always been this way.

There was once a time when you would find her laughing at her father's side, learning how to wield the bow and arrow, and hunt for her supper. Foraging in the snow was child's play to this hardy girl, for she was made of stern stuff, but she *always* had a smile upon her face.

Then one dark night the Aesir came, those thunderous gods from Asgard, charging through the mountains with power bristling at their hooves, and in an altercation that would prove fatal for the giant Thjazi, they stole her father's life away and left her lost and lonely.

In the blink of an eye, the girl who would be a giant in so many ways felt smaller than a flake of snow. And just like sudden snowfall, she was left adrift. But there is something you should know about living in extreme environments. It makes you strong. The daily battle against the elements shapes the will, it carves resolve, and births fortitude, and so it did in Skadi.

The girl rose up like a mountain of ice to greet the dawn, and when she took a breath, the landscape shook; and when she took a step, the heavens quivered. She donned her best and brightest armor and with helmet and spear in hand, she stepped from the world of giants into the realm of the gods. There was only one thing on her mind—revenge!

To say it took the gods by surprise belies the truth, for while Skadi was a mighty sight, she was still a woman, and not considered their equal. At first they laughed, but their guffaws were met with an icy stare and the promise of sudden death, and so, to avoid any needless bloodshed they offered her a gift by way of recompense.

"You can take any god to be your husband, but you must choose by looking only at his feet."

Now Skadi was no fool. She knew it was likely that the fairest of face would have the loveliest feet, and so she chose the perfect pair thinking they belonged to the handsome Baldur. Alas, the feet she'd fallen at were those of Njord, the much older god of the sea. Even so, the goddess had given her word, and it was as pure as the first snowfall in spring. She went to live with Njord in his watery kingdom and tried to make the best of it.

While many would have enjoyed the riches of the sea, and the attentive water nymphs on hand to serve and beautify, this was not the life for Skadi. She longed for the freedom of her snow-speckled hills, the smooth, white slopes, and the barren trees. Her heart ached for the mountains of home, and as much as she loved her husband, she had to be true to herself. Njord, too, tried to appease his wife by living in her world, but being an ocean lord he was like a fish out of water, and yearned for the briny deep. A truce was made, and they went their separate ways, despite the love that had grown between them.

Skadi had to follow her heart, to stride, and glide down the icy slopes, to hunt and run up the mountains; to feel the spectral touch of the wind stealing her breath and making her heart beat faster. She had to be true to herself, even if that meant living alone in a place where it was forever winter, and no other soul could bear the chill.

This was her choice.

Her freedom.

This was Skadi the giantess, the girl who rose like a mountain.

GODDESS AFFIRMATION

"I rise up with courage to face any challenge."

GODDESS RITUAL

Being true to yourself is one of Skadi's main themes. Even when the going gets tough, this goddess follows her heart and stands up for what she believes is right for her. She is resilient when faced with adversity, and her cool focus means she's able to deal with obstacles with confidence.

This ritual uses the element of water and ice, which is associated with this goddess, to help calm your mind and strengthen your resolve when you're feeling vulnerable.

You'll need a piece of quartz crystal, either a polished stone or a crystal point, some fresh water, and an ice tray.

* To start, place the quartz into a jug, and cover it with water. Quartz crystal is renowned for its healing powers; it also boosts vitality and strength.

* Pop the jug into a refrigerator overnight, so that the water can be infused with the crystal's energy.

* In the morning retrieve the jug and remove the quartz.

* Decant the water in equal amounts into the ice tray and pop in the freezer.

* Every morning take one or two lumps of ice and use it either in your morning coffee, juice, or smoothie.

* Take your time as you sip the drink. Consider Skadi's amazing tale, and how she met each challenge with courage. Think about ways in which you can adopt the same approach during the day ahead, for example, take a step back and a deep breath to calm your mind when faced with a problem at work, or use your goddess affirmation to instill self-belief and confidence.

* Carry the quartz crystal with you as a reminder that you have the power to deal with anything.

Rhiannon

Celtic Goddess of the Moon and Horses

THEMES
Patience, truth, forgiveness, compassion

"THE TRUTH WILL SET YOU FREE"

There once lived a handsome king called Pwyll. He governed a magical land called Dyfed, where anything was possible. Being fair of face, he caught the eye of many young maidens, but there was only one who stole his heart. While out riding one day, he crossed paths with the goddess Rhiannon on her glowing white steed. She galloped ahead, her green-gold robes flapping in the wind. In that moment, he fell head over heels. It wasn't just her enchanting beauty; there was a purity that shone from her soul, something he had never encountered before. He chased after her, but she was riding at such a speed he could not keep up. In the end he called out for her to stop. She tugged on the reins of her horse and came to a halt.

"My king," she said, smiling.

"Why did you run away from me?" he asked.

"I was not running. All you had to do was ask me to stop and I would have."

The king nodded, and immediately understood that Rhiannon was his, and together they would rule in harmony. The bond between them was such that in that moment their fates were sealed. The two were married, and there was much celebration in the kingdom. Soon after, Rhiannon gave birth to a beautiful baby boy and like both his parents, he was a joy to behold.

One night the unthinkable happened. While Rhiannon slept, she left a nurse in charge of her son, but the nurse fell into a deep slumber and when she awoke, the boy had disappeared from his cot. Fearful she would get the blame, she smeared puppy blood upon the sleeping Rhiannon's lips then accused the goddess of eating him. "She's a witch, a mistress of the moon, what do you expect!" the nurse cried, pointing at Rhiannon's bloody face.

The king looked at his stunning bride, and his heart ached for the loss of his son, but more than that, his pride had taken a tumble. For how could he not have seen this side to her? There was no other explanation, his child would not simply vanish into thin air, and Rhiannon was aligned to the moon's influence, which could indeed send her mad.

It didn't matter how much the goddess protested her innocence; the king would not hear it. She cried and begged, and wept at his feet, but it was to no avail. Despite her terrible crime, he still loved her and could not bring himself to kill her. Instead he banished her to the castle gates, and a life of pain and misery.

"You are no longer welcome here. You are wretched and disgusting and I do not wish to see you anymore. What you have done is despicable and you will spend the rest of your days confessing your crimes to anyone who visits the castle. Then you will carry them on your back up the hill to the castle entrance, like the pitiful pony that you are!" Rhiannon didn't argue. She could see that the king's mind was made up, and there was no way to change it. Instead she accepted her fate, and punishment, for a crime she had not committed. The nurse for her part kept her mouth shut and continued to console Pwyll for his loss.

Every day, Rhiannon would be forced to relive her shame by telling her story to all and sundry, as they jeered and mocked her. Then, she would carry any visitors and their belongings upon her back, up the rocky hill toward the castle. It was an arduous and painful task, and one that soon laid heavy upon her, but she did not complain or feel sorry for herself. Instead every night she would whisper to the moon, and cast her illuminating light upon the land in the hope of finding her son.

Eventually, as with all deceptions, the truth was revealed. The child was found, alive and well, and the nurse's lies were exposed. The family were reunited, and all of those who had poked a finger and laughed at the goddess were humbled. And while most would have enjoyed their discomfort and even punished those who had gone against them, Rhiannon forgave everyone. She forgave her people for their nasty jibes and the way they'd treated her. She forgave the nurse for lying and conjuring such a falsehood—she could see that the woman had been acting in fear. Most of all she forgave her husband, who should have believed her. All that mattered was the truth, and the truth had set her free. From that day forward Rhiannon reigned with compassion in her heart, and the light of the moon to protect her.

Rhiannon

"I set myself free, by forgiving myself and others."

GODDESS RITUAL

Gentle Rhiannon couldn't possibly have hurt her son. Her pure soul shines with compassion, and she acts with an open heart and mind. She is able to empathize with those who have done her wrong, and she urges you to do the same in your dealings with others. She knows that holding a grudge will cause more pain, and that forgiveness sets everyone free.

This ritual uses the illuminating light of the moon and Rhiannon's colors to help you release past hurts and let forgiveness flow.

You will need a white candle, a pen, and some paper.

✳ Light the white candle; this represents the illuminating light of the moon.

✳ Take the paper and pen to write a letter to yourself. Instead of holding on to guilt, forgive yourself; say, "I forgive myself for . . ." and then write a list.

✳ Let all your emotions spill onto the paper, then read what you have written with compassion in your heart.

✳ Imagine this is your dearest friend reaching out and asking for forgiveness.

✳ To finish, say, "I forgive me for everything. I am free to move forward." Take the paper and pass it through the flame, then let it burn to ash.

Lakshmi

Hindu Goddess of Wealth, Good Fortune, and Success

THEMES
Accomplishment, perfection, grace, effort

"THE TURNING OF THE TIDES"

There was a time when demons walked the earth, a time when it was not safe for humankind to inhabit the planet, and so the gods took it upon themselves to wage war with the demons, to eradicate them for good. During this fraught phase, there came a goddess more beautiful and bountiful than most, for she was the goddess Lakshmi. Such a being there had never been before. Everything about her was enchanting, and her only wish was to make the world a better place for everyone. Blessings poured from every pore, indeed every part of the goddess was loving and giving. And while she had the power to bestow wealth and good fortune, she did it all with grace, for to her, the most important part was seeing the delight it gave others. She was concerned with beauty in every form, from the sacred flowers that fell at her feet, to the handsome face of the great lord Vishnu, her cosmic consort and soulmate.

You might think that such a benevolent deity would have little to do with heavenly battles, and prefer calmer skies, but Lakshmi believed in what was right and good and she also believed in hard work. When the Hindu god Indra waged war against the demonic forces that plagued the earth, she stood by his side, prepared to fight in whatever way she could. In the midst of the battle, Indra callously discarded the sacred lotus flowers that Lakshmi loved so much, a slight that hurt her to the core and so she fled to the Milky Ocean, where she was submerged within the swirling depths.

As you might expect, this turn of events changed things, for wherever Lakshmi was there was light and goodness, and so without her these things ceased to exist. The world was plunged into never-ending darkness, the sky bled into

the earth, and the shadows spilled forth. The gods suffered loss after loss, and the demons thrived. All hope had gone, and the deities wondered if they would ever overcome the evil before them. It was Vishnu who finally came up with a plan.

"We must bring Lakshmi back, we must churn the Milky Ocean, over and over again, until we connect with her. She is the only one who can turn the tides of our fortunes and save us."

"But churning the ocean is no simple task," the deities cried.

Vishnu agreed. "It will be arduous; there will be effort required, but it will be worth it if it ensures our success."

So they traveled across space and time to the Milky Ocean, and they churned the waters, over and over again. They worked using all their might and energy, churning for several thousand years. Eventually, just when they thought that all their efforts had been futile, the oceans began to swirl and part. The treasures within the deep began to rise to the surface, floating upward into the arms of the gods. From gems that could only have been found on the ocean bed, to the elixir of life, a potion that granted the drinker immortality. All these things and more began to emerge. And then when the waters finally calmed, the goddess Lakshmi appeared, resplendent in a red dress, carrying in her hand a beautiful lotus bloom. She was even more captivating than in her previous incarnation.

As she rose to the surface to take her place by the side of Vishnu and the other deities, she brought with her every good thing that had ever been in the world, and every good thing that was to come. When she smiled the light poured from her; its brightness was blinding. Her blessings were innumerable and after all that work, the gods finally achieved success. The tides of fortune had been turned, the goddess Lakshmi unleashed her powers, and the demons were thwarted.

Once more the world was filled with goodness. The people experienced joy and abundance and praised the great goddess Lakshmi for her gifts. They realized, too, that just like the gods who had churned the Milky Ocean for thousands of years, if they put in the work and the effort, they would be rewarded. Lakshmi would see their devotion and repay them with success and riches beyond their wildest dreams. She would turn the tides on their fortunes, just as she had turned the tides all those years ago, when demons walked the earth.

"I turn the tides of my fate, with effort and grace."

GODDESS RITUAL

Beatific and benevolent, Lakshmi wants to bless her followers with abundance and good fortune, but she also believes that they must play their part. She rewards hard work with success and gives those who accept the twists and turns of fate with grace, a chance to start again.

This ritual works with one of Lakshmi's most popular symbols to help you generate good fortune, for yourself and others.

This goddess is almost always pictured holding a lotus bloom, and flowers of any kind are sacred to her, because they are beautiful and imbued with goodness. For this exercise you will need a pen and paper, and a bunch of your favorite flowers in bud.

* To start, think about what you'd like to create; what kind of good fortune do you want to generate? For example, perhaps you'd like a promotion at work, or some luck in love.

* Write a few sentences that encapsulate what you're hoping to achieve.

* Next, take the blooms and arrange them in a vase filled with water.

* Place the vase on top of the paper that lists your goals.

* Every day, change the water in the vase, arrange the flowers, and cut away any dead blooms. Spend time, care, and effort making them look nice.

* Make a point of repeating the goddess affirmation for Lakshmi each time you do this, to remind you that good things come to those who make the effort.

Aphrodite

Greek Goddess of the Sea, Love, and Beauty

THEMES
Love, self-assurance, passion, beauty

"THE GOLDEN APPLE OF DISCORD"

There was once a Greek goddess, more beautiful than all the rest, for she was the goddess of love. Everything about her was love, from the elegant way she held herself, to the graceful sway of her walk. Her smile set hearts alight, and her voice was smooth and powerful like the sea from which she was born. Fully formed, she stepped from the foam of the waves, gliding from the ocean, a beatific and voluptuous being. Her grace and presence were as calm and as passionate as the bountiful body of water that formed her essence. One look from this deity could cause lovers to swoon and passions to bloom, and should you get lost in her eyes, there was no escape—you would be floating like a love-sick fool for an eternity.

You might think being the goddess of love was a pure delight, after all it is universal, and what could be more lovely than to govern the fairest of emotions, but the truth is Aphrodite was easily bored. While she had many dalliances herself, she also loved to matchmake and enjoyed meddling in the affairs of men and gods. In truth, while her intentions were genuine most of the time, she liked to play games, to throw lovers together and cause chaos for her own amusement. And should any man best her, or cheat in any way, then Aphrodite would use the power of love as her revenge.

One such man who learned this to his cost was the King of Sparta, Menelaus. He made a deal with the goddess in return for winning the hand of his beautiful wife Helen, but then reneged on his agreement to give her a herd of his cattle. It never does to anger the gods and Aphrodite was deadly when provoked, so in a bid to make him pay for his slight she plotted to steal away the one thing he prized more

than his worldly goods—his new bride.

Never one to miss an opportune moment, Aphrodite saw her chance to take revenge during a frivolous game with the other deities. It started with an apple, the simplest and sweetest of fruit, but of course in the realm of the gods nothing is quite as it seems. This was no ordinary gift from the orchard; it was a golden apple, and had been cast into the garden by the goddess of discord, Eris. Upon it was written one phrase; "To the fairest," three little words that were sure to start a squabble among the many heavenly beauties.

It was down to Zeus, as father of the gods, to choose. He was the most powerful and greatest of them all, and he was not stupid. To pick only one, to make such a decision, would surely incur the bitterness of the others. So he did what any good god would do in a tricky situation— he delegated.

The young prince Paris would do the choosing. The three goddesses who laid claim to the title were Aphrodite, Hera, and Athena. Each one offered Paris a gift should he choose them, and while power and wisdom were tempting, they were not enough to sway the boy.

Aphrodite was last to state her case, and taking her time, she looked deep into the prince's eyes and saw his soul and in that moment, she knew that what he wanted most in the world was love. This was something only she could give him.

"For you my lord, I promise you may have the hand in marriage of the most beautiful woman in the world; her name is Helen of Sparta," she said.

And so the die was cast, and a deal was struck, and the golden apple was soon in the slender hand of Aphrodite. While she graciously accepted the accolade, her smile must surely have been for what she knew was to come. In that instant the strands of fate came together, just as she had planned. Paris abducted Helen, whisking her away to Troy and what ensued was a grisly battle as King Menelaus fought to reclaim his bride. If only he'd honored his deal, but humans were fickle and selfish.

As Aphrodite looked on from her seat in the heavens, she nodded in amusement; everything had worked out perfectly. Of course, when the other deities asked what her part in this had been, she claimed innocence. After all, this could be nothing to do with her! She was the goddess of love and beauty; how could she be responsible for a war?

Instead she would refer to the golden apple, and say, "Such a sweet fruit, it shall forever be known as the golden apple of discord."

"I am love, I give love, I receive love, I love myself."

GODDESS RITUAL

Aphrodite may appear cunning in this tale, but she believes that what she does is for the greater good, and she believes in herself. This self-assurance allows her to blossom, and her natural allure shines from within. She can help you learn to love yourself, and in turn, open your heart to others.

This ritual, which looks at your self-image, will help to boost self-esteem and generate loving energy.

It's best if you can get into the habit of performing this ritual at the same time every day, for example in the morning before you leave for work, or in the evening before bed.

✳ Stand in front of a full-length mirror and spend a few minutes looking at your reflection. The mirror is one of Aphrodite's symbols, and she was not averse to gazing at herself!

✳ Take a deep breath in, and, as you exhale, imagine a thread of light coming out of the top of your head, which tugs gently upward, lengthening your spine.

✳ Roll your shoulders back and balance your weight equally between both feet.

✳ Continue to breathe deeply and look into your eyes. Connect with your inner goddess and see the beauty within.

✳ Smile—even if you don't feel like it, force yourself to smile and you should notice your feelings gradually changing. Notice also how the smile lights up your face.

✳ Say, while still gazing into your eyes, "I am beautiful, I love myself."

A Final Word

The stories in this book have been created to take you on a journey, to introduce you to the wonderful world of goddesses, and show how they might help and inspire you. Each one has a message, and a role to play, but this will be distinctly different for everyone. Stories are unique, as is your response to them, just as each deity is unique, and there will be some you like more than others.

Like people, you'll find it easier to connect with some characters, and you'll instantly click and understand where they're coming from. Then there are the personalities who you can't seem to get a handle on, the ones who make you feel uncomfortable. These are just as important, for they teach you something about yourself, and ask you to address issues that you might otherwise have avoided. Whatever your response, there is joy to be found within these pages, and also sisterhood. There is enlightenment and encouragement, and most of all there is a calling here. By understanding the deeper themes at work, you'll be able to connect with the divine feminine within and step into your own power.

Further Reading

Warriors, Witches, Women by Kate Hodges, White Lion Publishing

Encyclopaedia of Goddesses and Heroines by Patricia Monaghan, New World Publishing

Be Your Own Goddess by Kirsten Riddle, CICO Books

Evolution of Goddess by Emma Mildon, Atria/Enliven Books

Acknowledgments

I would like to thank my amazing editor Chloe Murphy, who I know has magic at her fingertips when she shapes and crafts each book, and the fabulous team at Leaping Hare Press for helping to put this together. I would also like to thank the illustrator Katja for her wonderful illustrations, which really bring the tales to life and accentuate the beauty of each goddess. Thanks, too, to the brilliant copy editor Imogen, who polished the writing with the lightest of touches. Finally I would like to say thank you to all of the goddesses out there—the fabulous women who help to make, shape, and create this world. You are DIVINE.

Disclaimer

Index

First published in 2023 by Leaping Hare Press,
an imprint of The Quarto Group.
1 Triptych Place, London
SE1 9SH
United Kingdom
T (0)20 7700 6700
www.Quarto.com

A catalogue record for this book is
available from the British Library.

ISBN 978-0-7112-8324-4

Ebook ISBN 978-0-7112-8326-8

10 9 8 7 6 5 4 3 2 1

Design by Georgie Hewitt
Text by Alison Davies
Illustrations by Katja Perez
Production Controller: Maeve Healy
Commissioning Editor: Chloe Murphy
Edited by Katerina Menhennet

Printed in China

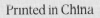